Skira Guides

Skira Guides

Palazzo Te Mantua

Edited by
Ugo Bazzotti

Cover
Façade on the Fisheries; Chamber
of Amore and Psyche; Loggia of David

Design
Marcello Francone

Editing
Elena Bajetta

Layout
Sara Salvi

Translations
Isobel Butters

Photographs
Mauro Magliani, Padova
Mauro Ranzani, Olgiate Olona

Plans and Maps
Studio Margil, Certosa di Pavia

Perspective Drawing
Luciano Boschini, Milano

First published in Italy in 2007 by
Skira Editore S.p.A.
Palazzo Casati Stampa
via Torino 61
20123 Milano
Italy
www.skira.net

© 2007 by Skira editore

Printed and bound in Italy. First edition

Contents

Introduction

Place and Name

In its descent towards the Po, the Mincio river, which has its source in lake Garda, "soon encounters a mire into which it stretches and becomes a swamp", as Dante explains. Mantua evolved in the middle of four lakes formed by the river. A "shot of the crossbow" away, was another smaller island called *Teieto* (hence *Tè*), connected by a bridge to the southern walls of the city. We can imagine it verdant, quiet and protected by rare buildings.

It soon became the recreation place of the Gonzaga family. In 1459 marquis Ludovico II took guests to see a female leopard running there, and his wife Barbara of Brandenburg, in 1480, stated: "We keep the place of the Te for our pleasure". Isabella d'Este, in 1492, writes to a court official that she wishes "to have live hares to cook at the Te, a place surrounded by water, where we wish sometimes to relax". At the beginning of the sixteenth century the husband of Isabella, Francesco II, had spacious stables built on the island for his celebrated and adored thoroughbred horses, and provided these stables with a manor house. The frescoes that came to light in the attic, one of which is dated 1502, and in other parts of the northern wing of the present villa, belonged to an important building. The name of the island has often given rise to spurious etymologies. As suggested by Luzio at the start of the twentieth century, similarly to other like-sounding place names, the medieval *Teieto* may derive from *tiglieto*, place of lime-trees, or be connected to *tezza, tegia*, from *atteggia*, a Latin word meaning hut.

A Palazzo for the Honest Leisure of the Prince

Long awaited, Giulio Romano arrived at the Mantuan court in October 1524, where he stayed, in the service of marquis Federico II, son of

Francesco II and Isabella d'Este. The meeting between the two and his subsequent commission to build Palazzo Te is evocatively described by Vasari, who received the information directly from Giulio while in Mantua in 1541: "[Baldassarre Castiglione] introduced him to the marquis who, after many caresses, ordered him to be given an honourably furnished house and ordered a salary for him [...] And afterwards, learning that he had no horse, ordered Luggieri, one of his favourites, to be brought, gave it to him, and when Giulio was mounted, they left through the S. Bastiano gate, a shot of the crossbow away, to a site where his Excellency had a place and some stables called the T(e) in the midst of a meadow where he kept his thoroughbred stallions and mares. And once there, the marquis said he would like, without spoiling the old walls, to build a small residence to which he could retire sometimes to feast, or dine for pleasure. [...] This caused the fact that, from a modest beginning, the marquis decided to make the whole building like a grand palazzo; Giulio made a wonderful model, all outside and in the courtyard of the rustic part. His lordship liked it so much that he ordered a good supply of money and Giulio was brought a great many master craftsmen. The work did not take long". The reasons for building the villa are expressed in writing in the chamber of Psyche; it is a palazzo for free time, for the "honesto ocio", honest leisure, of the prince, who in truth did not use it often, preferring the villa at Marmirolo for his holidays. However, Federico and his descendents used it for entertaining important guests, such as the Holy Roman Emperor and king of France, Charles V. The king stayed at Palazzo Te twice, in 1530 and 1532. News about his first stay and the rooms he visited will be provided on the visit.

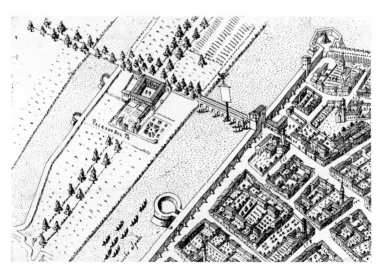

Urbis Mantuae Descriptio. Perspective plan by Gabriele Bertazzolo, 1628. Detail with Palazzo Te

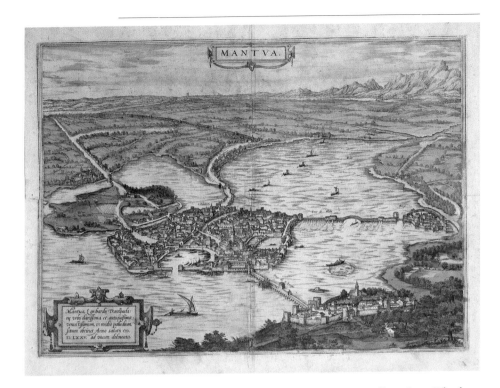

Mantua.
Perspective plan by
Braun-Hogenberg,
1575

The palazzo underwent the ravages of man as well as time. The lansquenets occupied Mantua, sacking it in 1630 and remaining until spring of the following year. They invaded the undefended palazzo and their signatures, dated 1631, are scratched on the frescoes in the room of the Giants. During the eighteenth century, after the fall of the Gonzaga, the Austrian government used part of the villa as a barracks. Animals, army baggage and materials were piled everywhere, soldiers were quartered even in the decorated rooms and the gardens were used for cannon practice. At the time of Maria Teresa, the government decided to save the rundown villa and turned to the recently founded Accademia di Belle Arti to restore the walls and decorations. In the Napoleonic period changes, considered improvements at the time, were made to the southern wing, but shortly afterwards the building was once again taken over by the military and once again it fell into decline. In 1876, the State sold it to the Municipality, who gradually restored it and opened it up to the public. During the 1980s, the Municipality, Monuments and Fine Arts Office and the Istituto Centrale del Restauro again began a new wave of renovation and study which culminated in 1989 with the greatly successful Giulio Romano exhibition. In 1998 Amedeo Belluzzi published an extensive mono-

9

graphic work on Palazzo Te which plays an essential role in understanding the building and is a great help for future studies.

The Patron

Federico Gonzaga was born in 1500 and died in 1540. One of his greatest achievements was the war campaign of 1522 during which, busy defending Pavia from the French army, he saw himself as a modern David fighting against Goliath. To Guicciardini, "the marquis of Mantua is not worth much", but, he adds, as a condottiere he "advised well". Perhaps aware of his limits, Federico soon retired from his role as a soldier, despite the titles he obtained as Captain General of the Church

Tiziano Vecellio, *Portrait of Federico II Gonzaga*, Madrid, Prado

and Florentine Republic, to dedicate himself to governing the state and his own personal interests. Predominant among these was his love for art and classical objects. In this he showed himself to be the spiritual heir and imitator of his mother, Isabella d'Este, a refined patron and collector. We also know that his father, Francesco II, seemingly less receptive than his wife, was a fine patron to Mantegna and that he built palazzo San Sebastiano. A treasure trove of art, it was a Gonzaga residence just beyond the southern limits of the city that foreshadowed and contributed to the design of Palazzo Te. Looking back at the lineage of forefathers we encounter Ludovico II, whom Mantegna and Alberti both worked under; Gianfrancesco, the patron of Pisanello; Francesco I, at whose court were Pierpaolo and Iacomello dalle Masegne. Federico II welcomed and fostered this inheritance, fully aware that his role as prince of a small state, despite his lack of ability as a military leader, could shine thanks to the splendour of court life shown off by the creative talent of the greatest artists. Absolute power over the state was in his hands from 1519, but he had already accumulated exceptional experiences. The first was between 1510 and 1513, when for political reasons he was held as a hostage at the papal court where he breathed the thrillingly new atmosphere of the Sistine chapel and Vatican Rooms; the second came during a long stay

(January 1516 – March 1517) at the French court, where he befriended the young sovereign and led a wonderfully exciting life, even finding a way of handing out much appreciated gifts: perfumes, gloves and model-dolls dressed in the latest fashion, all made by his unrivalled mother, Isabella. When Raphael died in 1520, the Gonzaga ambassador in Rome, Baldassarre Castiglione, took care to arrange for his most established pupils, Giulio Romano and Gianfrancesco Penni, to be sent to Mantua. For several years the two, heirs of Raphael's workshop, stayed in Rome to terminate their numerous commissions. Meanwhile, only Giulio confirmed that he was willing to take up residence at the Gonzaga court. Federico explained his dream to Giulio, and he, who designs "buildings […] that seem not dwellings for mankind, but houses for the gods, for example, made by men", does not disappoint him, since from a "modest beginning" he creates one of Europe's most greatly admired works of architecture.

The Artist and Planning of the Work
Giulio di Piero Pippi de' Iannuzzi, called Romano, was born in Rome on an uncertain date. His death certificate, written on November 1st 1546, says he was 47 years old; according to Vasari, instead, his date of birth was 1492. Most scholars accept the date on the document, justifying the success that so rapidly smiled on Giulio at Raphael's workshop, where he was entrusted with important tasks from 1515 onwards, to his early genius and versatility. Giulio was not only an important assistant on the painting, but also learnt to "throw into perspective, measure buildings and work ground plans". In Rome he had already given early proof of his skills as an architect and before arriving in Mantua he sent a model for a new building in Marmirolo, so beautiful it was thought to be a "design by Michelangelo". Unlike other fellow pupils he did not simply rework Raphael's teaching but also looked at the art of Michelangelo, to whom he pays homage at Palazzo Te in the dynamism of his compositions, gigantic figures, accentuated anatomy and expressive power. Giulio was clever at interpreting the wishes of his patrons, gifted as he was with a readiness and originality of invention that amazed his contemporaries and ranged from planning the urban area to the single building, from stucco work to painting, temporary celebratory apparatus, tapestries and silverware. Vasari goes on to comment: "and although he was almost always used in great works, it is not that he did not turn his hand to much smaller things to serve his lordship and friends, and no sooner had one opened one's mouth to express an idea than he had already understood and drawn it […] To him drawing was like writing endlessly".

His success at the court of Mantua was immediate and lasting. His commissions were numerous and often overlapped, and soon he was formally named Prefect of the Works. Besides the Gonzaga buildings— the Te, the Castle, Marmirolo—he was also active in city life, more so than any other court artist of the past. As Head of the Roads he solved problems relating to the marshy nature of the streets and quarters, and he watched over private building projects: no one can "build in that city without Giulio's instructions". He also carried out notable works in its religious architecture, with plans for the cathedral of Mantua and the basilica of San Benedetto in Polirone. Vasari, asked for an opinion by Cardinal Ercole Gonzaga, state regent on the death of Federico II, remarks that the works by Giulio "were so many that every corner of the city should bear his statue; as he had renovated it (the city) half of the state would not be enough to repay the efforts and virtues of Giulio. To which the cardinal replied that Giulio was more owner of the state than he was".

The act of creation starts and ends with his drawings, which provided the source for his assistants, as the court officials well knew: "Master Iulio has so much to do, to tell the truth, in drawing and giving work to so many men who all live by his bread" that "he has no time to hurry them on, other than giving a quick look every day". The social role of the Prefect of the Works becomes more important than the subordinate position as a simple "court artist", who acquires merit through the work of his own hands. His ideas, set down on paper, are assigned to others who materially execute them. Under the Gonzaga, artistic creation had already obtained exceptional recognition when Mantegna was given the status of a nobleman, and on August 31st 1526 Giulio Romano too was made a court deputy. The formal decree specifies that the nomination is assigned following proof of his skills and integrity: "satis iam exploratam habentes sufficientiam et integritatem dilectissimi civis nostri Iulii Pipi romani". This is another reason why Giulio does not physically execute the decorations, but in response to a stiff reprimand from Federico for the slowness of the work in the chamber of Psyche, he ironically suggests he should be personally involved: "if it pleases you, shut me in that room until it is finished". We also know from Vasari that he contributed a series of important finishing touches to this room to improve the quality, but it was the exception rather than the rule. On another occasion, because the Castle site was subject to a slowdown due to "the intolerable heat", flooding and sickness among the workers, he underlines the fact that he personally transferred the drawings on to life-size cartoons, essential for applying the fresh intonaco: "about the room I made the

cartoons because the painters themselves had no time to do them". Giulio Romano applied the working model learnt at Raphael's workshop, keeping tight control over invention, which was unfailingly attributed to him. He is the creator and director of the entire oeuvre, from spatial to architectonic composition and from the large-scale works to the most minute decoration. This is the environment in which his assistants move, and the reason for the stimulating critical studies still directed at singling out his individual contributions within the general unity of this immense structure.

Palazzo Te

The Exterior

Records testify to how the term "palazzo" goes back a long way, although it is better suited to defining the major buildings in an urban context. It is the experts' considered opinion that Palazzo Te was inspired by the ancient villa, the nobleman's country residence, the importance of which was to exploit the relationship with "the horizontal views of the gardens and the fountains, and the other things that please the eye", according to Scamozzi's theory. So Palazzo Te, with its square plan and large courtyard in the centre, has very long sides (about 65 metres) and the first floor is slightly elevated above the surrounding ground to protect it from flooding by the Mincio; the servants' quarters are upstairs. In town the opposite is true: the ground floor is for the servants and the master rooms, to which access is gained via important staircases, are on the first floor. The layout of the façade reflects Giulio's choice, with large windows on the ground floor and smaller ones, distributed unevenly, on the first floor. The impression of a solid whole emerges due to the use of the single order, with Doric pillars that punctuate the surfaces and horizontal elements—string course cornice and entablature—that tighten the volumes. The north façade, seen as the visitor approaches from the city, and the west one, which one gradually catches sight of as one draws closer, stand on a smooth podium on which the base of simulated rustic ashlar-work is surmounted by smooth ashlar; however, this surface too is broken up by the rustic window frames. Despite the unitary and homogeneous appearance, the façades reveal understandable conceptual differences, such as the single arch to the west, and the loggia with its three arches to the north. The first, flanked by two pairs of pilasters, is the main entrance; the second provides a view and connects exterior and inte-

Axonometric view
of Palazzo Te

Legenda
1. Courtyard
of Honour
2. Hall of the Horses
3. Chamber
of Psyche
4. Loggia of David
5. Chamber
of the Giants
6. Fisheries
7. Fruttiere
8. Exedra
9. Secret Garden
10. Grotto

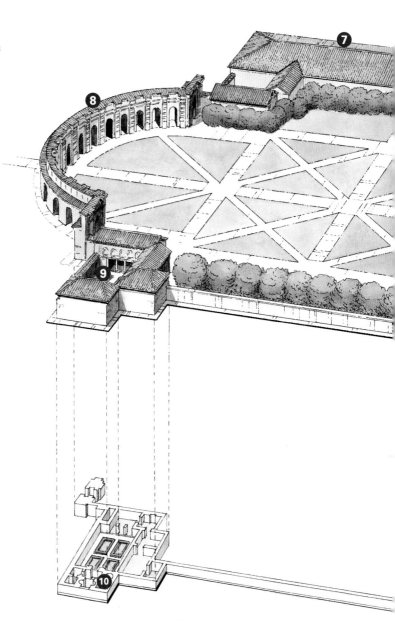

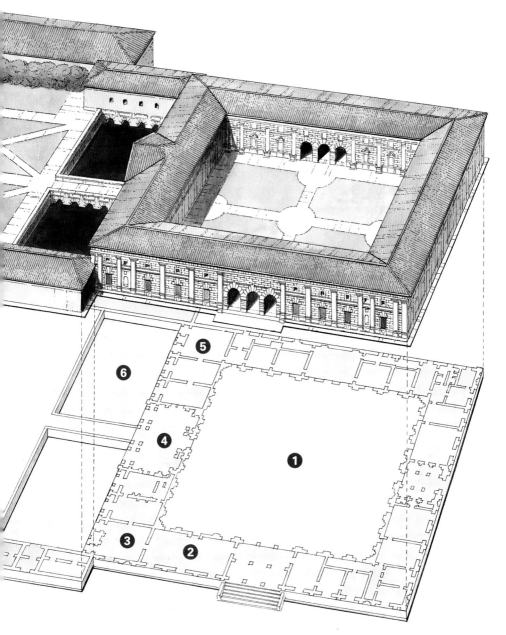

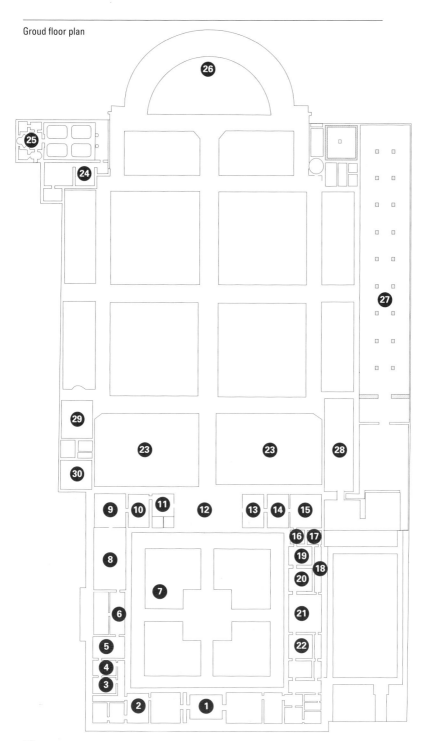

First floor plan

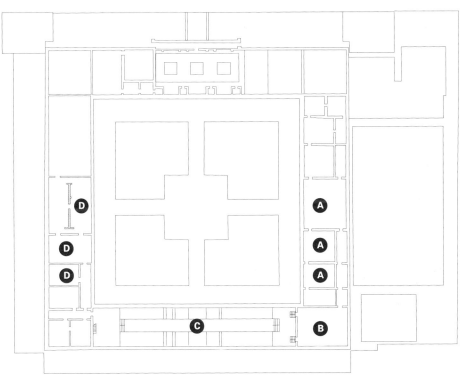

Groud floor
1. Entrance
2. Chamber of Tiziano
3. Chamber of Ovid
4. Chamber of the Devices
5. Chamber of the Sun and the Moon
6. Loggia of the Muses
7. Courtyard of Honour
8. Hall of the Horses
9. Chamber of Psyche
10. Chamber of the Winds
11. Chamber of the Eagles
12. Loggia of David
13. Chamber of the Stuccoes
14. Chamber of the Emperors
15. Chamber of the Giants
16. Small Cross Vault Chamber
17. Small Chamber of Grotesques
18. Small Chamber of Venus
19. Chamber of the Candelabra
20. Chamber of the Caryatids
21. South Loggia
22. Chamber of the Victories
23. Fisheries
24. Apartment of the Secret Garden
25. Grotto
26. Exedra
27. Fruttiere
28. Auditorium or Polyvalent Hall
29. Exit and Bookstore
30. Cafeteria

First floor
A. "Arnoldo Mondadori" Donation
B. "Ugo Sissa" Mesopotamic Collection
C. Sezione Gonzaghesca
D. "Giuseppe Acerbi" Egyptian Collection

rior, which was particularly important when that side of the villa had a walled garden beside it. Other differences are less easily explained. The metopes on the north side are decorated with a series of Gonzaga devices that do not appear on the other façades; the continual asymmetry can only be slightly, or is completely unjustified, by restrictions caused by pre-existing structures, or by the layout of the rooms inside. In the apparent unity of the whole, striking in the size and dignity of its conception, Giulio hides and at the same time reveals liberties and deceptions, freeing himself of the formal and repetitive metrics of the classicists. The other two elevations are very different. The east façade for reasons of planning; the unfinished south side (not included in the visit), has flat intonaco facing, with traces of simulated architecture, probably added later.

The Atrium

The entrance provides us with the main view of the palazzo and lies parallel to the entrance of the David loggia in the centre of the east façade of the courtyard of Honour. In front of us is the garden, enclosed at the far end in 1651 by a spectacular exedra. The atrium that greets the visitor has a tripartite rectangular ground plan that "is an interpretation of the *atrium* of the *domus* by Vitruvius popular in Rome in the early sixteenth century" (Belluzzi). The central barrel vault decorated with octagonal coffers inspired by those in the basilica of Maxentius, is supported by four columns with roughly-hewn shafts and detailed base and capital. Made of cut stone, they provide an example of all the rusticated surfaces at the palazzo, sculpted to look like shafts roughly outlined in the quarry. The interplay between real and imitation stone, between natural reality and artifice establishes itself at once with the rustic pilasters, the stucco surfaces that, alternating with alcoves, punctuate the walls in a tribute to the dynamic articulation of imperial architectures. The barrel vault in the atrium is uniquely flanked by two flat ceilings with square coffers. The stone step running all the way round, which also serves as a seat, extends the existence and sense of the podium on which the palazzo is built. The west wing, with the main entrance, has no decorations and generally housed the kitchen and pantry. To the right of the atrium are two rooms that in the sixteenth century were described as "small public dining room" and "private dining room for the officers"; they were clearly where the prince's staff would eat. Nowadays they are chiefly used for exhibitions.

Ticket Office and Chamber of Titian

After leaving the ticket office, entered through the left bay of the atrium, there is a room with information panels and a modern wooden model (1981) of the present day layout of the building, including adjoining buildings and the exedra. Behind glass is Titian's *Portrait of Giulio Romano*. Titian was communicating with Federico Gonzaga between 1522 and 1540, and from 1536 his relationship with the

The atrium

Mantuan court intensified as he was involved in a series of paintings of *Caesars* for the Ducal Palace. Giulio Romano, with whom he had become friendly, is portrayed in a three quarters profile holding up the ground plan of an ancient building, or the project for an unidentified religious building with a central plan. The painting is refined and restrained: the black clothes, finely delineated in grey, are barely distinguishable from the dark background that is lightened slightly towards the outlines of the figure by thin layers of green earth. The light focuses on the sitter's face and hands, which are thrown into sharp contrast with the white of the collar, cuffs and white sheet of paper. The work is historically documented in Giulio Romano's house and later in the Gonzaga collections. Then, following the fate of many works sold by the Gonzaga to Charles I of England, it became part of the royal collection and was exhibited in Whitehall. Later sold privately, it was auctioned for the first time in 1946, after which it changed hands on various occasions, remaining for over a decade in the collection of Philippine dictator, Ferdinand Marcos. It came up for sale again in 1996 when it finally became public property thanks to the Province of Mantua and Lombardia Region, who purchased it for Palazzo Te. It is interesting to compare the painted portrait with the one given by Vasari in his *Lives*: "Giulio was neither tall nor short, more stocky than slight, dark-skinned, handsome, with lively dark eyes, extremely likeable, always polite, a small eater, simple dresser and honourable in his way of life".

Chamber of Ovid, or of the Metamorphoses

This is the first decorated room we come to, although it is the second room of an apartment whose entrance is the chamber of the Sun and the Moon. Briefly documented, it was one of the first decorated rooms: in 1527 stucco worker Andrea di Pezi was paid for having "worked on a fireplace in one of the small rooms, in the part of the palace near the city". The red Verona marble fireplace has a stucco hood made to look like marble and the device of Olympus at the top. A dedication on the architrave reads: F<edericus> II G<onzaga> M<archio> M<antuae> V: Federico second Gonzaga fifth marquis of Mantua. The painted decoration occupies the frieze, leaving the lower part of the walls bare to ac-

Chamber of Ovid,
*Orpheus
in Underworld*

22

commodate luxurious fabrics or Cordovan leather hangings here, as in most of the rooms of the villa. A source of inspiration is the classical decoration the artists in Rome went to study in the "grottoes" of the Oppio hill, where the ruins buried by the *Domus Aurea* lay. Immediately prior to this decoration is cardinal Bibbiena's *Stufetta* in the Vatican: panels with landscapes and mythological stories and panels of imitation marble. The landscapes are imaginary, apart from the one to the right of the window which shows a view of the island of the Te, with the palazzo still under construction: it is a fleeting vision, almost as if it were part of a play of mirrors. Starting from the entrance wall and proceeding to the right, the subjects inspired by mythology are: *Orpheus in the Underworld; The Punishment of Marsia*. This painting inspired the magnificent work by Titian of the same subject in Kroměříž, Moravia. *The Judgement of Paris; Bacchus and Ariadne; Dancing satyrs and maenads; The contest between Apollo and Pan; Dionysius drunk; Maenads tormenting a satyr.* Near the window under the wooden moulding a small area of the layer underneath can be seen. Dating to 1502 and closely connected to Mantegna's style it belongs to a decorative tradition derived from classical modelling. Giulio's slender and brightly coloured plant shoots demonstrate the effect that direct knowledge of Roman painting and the discovery of classical colours had on the art of the Cinquecento. The room was still being lived in as recently as the early part of the twentieth century, a fact which contributed to the damage of the original ceiling.

Chamber of the Devices

Similar in spatial layout and decoration to the previous room, the chamber takes its name from the main subject in the frieze: an anthology of "imprese", devices of the Gonzaga. The device is an emblem made up of an image (*body*) and, almost always, by a motto. Born in the Middle Ages, the fashion for devices spread in the Renaissance, partly due to the publication of a treatise on the subject, and it continued into the seventeenth and eighteenth centuries. The device could express the values of the person who adopted it, or historical events that happened to them, or amorous secrets represented enigmatically. According to Paolo Giovio, the device should not be so explicit as to be understood by everyone, nor entirely obscure, but it should arouse the curiosity of a person of culture: this is why the mottoes are almost always expressed in a different language—ancient or modern— from the person who adopts the device. The emblems are handed down from father to son and can be "given" to dear and faithful friends. Not to be confused with heraldic shields, composed by sovereign conces-

sion and connected to the family, the device is "worn" by noblemen, military men, ladies, prelates and men of letters, who can create and exhibit them in large numbers. In this room, the Gonzaga shield with its four eagles (the original black has disappeared) appears in the centre of the wall opposite the window. The devices that surround it are below described and are linked to the lord who ordered them or the period in which they were adopted.

Wall Opposite the Window
1. Device of the *sun*. Second half of the fourteenth century.
Body: shining sun.
Motto: PAR UN DESIR, or PER UN DISIR.
Meaning: unknown.

2. Gonzaga shield.
3. Device of the *salamander*. Federico II.

Body: salamander (or green lizard).

Motto: QUOD HUIC DEEST ME TORQUET (what she lacks torments me).

Meaning: Federico's hot-blooded passion contrasted with the salamander, a cold-blooded animal that bears fire without consequence. It is often depicted on the fireplaces in the villa.

Wall Opposite the Fireplace
4. Device of the *boschetto*. Federico II.

Body: Amor holding a green tree and a dry one and blocking the path leading to the small wood in the background.

Motto: none.

Meaning: it is based on the surname of Federico's *favorita*, Isabella Boschetti, or Boschetto. The life (the green tree) or death (the dry tree) of the lover depends on access to the *boschetto*, a small wood, which Amor (love) can allow or deny.
5. Device of the *crucible*. Francesco II.

Body: a crucible among flames, containing a sheaf of gold bars.

Motto: PROBASTI DOMINE (Lord, you have tried me).

Meaning: Francesco II adopts this device after being accused of lacking determination in battle. His loyalty is tried like the gold in the goldsmith's melting pot.
6. Device of the *wings* (*lure?*). Late fourteenth century.

Body: two wings terminating in claws clasping a ring; perhaps the lure used by falconers to call the falcon.

Motto: none.

Meaning: uncertain; loyalty?
7. Device of the *turtle dove*. Gianfrancesco.

Body: a turtle dove on a dry, bent branch, in a puddle of murky water.

Motto: vrai amour ne se change (true love does not change)

Meaning: the turtle dove, faithful in life and even beyond as it sits on dry branches and drinks only muddy water after the death of its mate so that its reflected image does not remind it of its former companion.
8. Device of the *glove*. Ludovico II.

Body: an iron glove from a suit of armour.

Motto: BUENA FE NO ES MUDABLE (good faith cannot change)

Meaning: loyalty.

Window Wall
9. Device of the *dog*. Gianfrancesco.

Body: a seated dog with a muzzle.

Motto: DONEC (until when).

Meaning: loyalty; connection with the motto uncertain.

10. Device of the *firedog*. Federico II.

Body: firedog.

Motto: LICET (legitimate).

Meaning: the firedog does not burn amid the flames: a reference to love similar to that of the salamander?

Fireplace Wall

11. Device of the *belt*. From Charles VI de Valois, King of France. It was bought from the Bourbons and reached the Gonzaga through Chiara, daughter of Federico I, who married Gilberto di Montpensier.

Body: a knotted belt.

Motto: ESPERANCE (hope).

Meaning: the device, created to mark the occasion of a vow made to the Virgin Mary absolved by Charles VI, has not been deciphered. The belt is however attributed to the Virgin.

12. Device of *Mount Olympus*, or *Olympus*. Federico II.

Body: a mount with an uphill path; on the top is an altar decorated with a small log.

Motto: FIDES—OLYMPOS (faith—Olympus).

Meaning: faith, loyalty. On mount Olympus, spared of all bad weather, the ashes from sacrifices to the gods remain as an unchanging symbol of faith.

13. Device of the *muzzle*. Francesco II.

Body: muzzle.

Motto: CAUTIUS (with greater caution).

Meaning: the muzzle is a reminder of reserve, to uncommunicativeness as a sign of loyalty.

14. Device unidentified. Federico II.

Body: a partite shield (divided vertically into two). In the first half, two gold figures on a black field, a curved log and two U-shaped, handle-like logs; in the second half a black rod (vertical strip) on a light blue field.

Motto: none.

Meaning: unknown.

15. Device of the *tower*. Ludovico II.

Body: a tower surrounded by waves.

Motto: none.

Meaning: resoluteness, resistance to adversities?

The scrolls surrounding the devices are held up by putti enveloped in large, brightly coloured plant volutes; painted in the lower register are simulated encrustations of fine marble. The red marble fire-

Chamber of the
Devices. Detail
of the frieze
with the device
of the crucible

place has a central ornamental design flanked by volutes also in Verona marble but lighter in shade; it bears the same dedication as the one in the previous room.

Chamber of the Sun and the Moon

The high walls of this small room, which led to the apartment of the Metamorphoses, are scattered with eighteenth century relief work, casts of ancient marble originals (sides of sarcophagi in the centre of the long walls) and stucco work housed in other parts of the palazzo. The cornice and pavilion vault with flat surface above it are original. Much admired and imitated by other sixteenth century artists is the central panel, which resembles a long window on to the sky with the sun chariot descending and the moon chariot rising, a metaphor for the unceasing passing of time. The fresco, drawn by Giulio, has long been considered the work of his most brilliant apprentice: Francesco Primaticcio. Although there is no documentary evidence, the quality of the work and the interest subsequently shown by Primaticcio in copies and variations of the preparatory drawing do not contradict the idea. The webbing in the vault is divided into 192 panels (128 lozenges and 64 triangles) containing figures of men, animals and emblems. The network of descending lozenges is taken from a Raphaelesque motif used in the small vaults of the Vatican Loggias and an erudite reference to the apse of the classical temple of Venus in Rome. Most of the stucco relief-work, on a light blue background, also derives from a classical repertoire: coins, which Giulio himself collected, and gems; however there is no shortage of allusions to works by Raphael and Michelangelo, such as details from the cartoon of the *Battle of Casci-*

Chamber of the Sun and the Moon. The vault

Chamber of the Sun and the Moon. A detail of the vault

na, for instance. The repertoire used for the triangles at the sides of the composition is simpler and includes the devices of Olympus and the salamander, Federico's favourites, present in almost all the rooms. In the absence of specific records, it would seem reasonable to date the work between 1527–1528, in line with the other decorative work in this wing. The presence of various hands is made clear by the stylistic differences in the realisation of the drawings provided by Giulio; the major stuccoists on site probably worked here side by side: Nicolò da Milano, Giovan Battista Mantovano and Primaticcio himself, to whom the figures modelled with the most finely balanced composition and formal sensitivity are attributed.

Courtyard of Honour

After leaving the Chamber of the Sun and the Moon one reaches the loggia of the Muses and the eye is once again caught by the magnificent courtyard of Honour, to which the guests were led directly from the entrance hall. Their reception could not have been more stately or more impressive. The single order that characterises the four walls gives an overall sense of majesty, uniting all the elements of the vast and varied composition. The visitor, following the surge of the Doric half-columns, encounters, on the wall opposite the entrance, an entab-

28

lature with an architrave decorated with drops and a frieze conceived with the classical alternation of tryglyphs and metopes. But he or she discovers that from time to time, a tryglyph has slipped down, giving the apparently stable composition a sudden and unexpected sense of instability. In the metopes, relief work of weapons, jars and other objects (even footwear), executed by Benedetto di Bertoldo, called il Pretino, and Andrea de Conti (1533) alternates with masks with their mouths open wide: before the eighteenth century alterations to the roof, these spouted with rainwater. Originally, the pitch of the roof was hidden by an attic frescoed in chiaroscuro by Fermo da Caravaggio, with plant friezes, small putti and exotic animals. The composition is on the whole mirrored in the one on the opposite wall, with noticeable differences, such as the portals on the east and west sides, and in the layout of the half-columns to the north and south. The rustication that frames or flanks the windows on the lower floor stands out amid the decoration of smooth ashlar. The classical tympana of the windows seems contrived as a result of the violent addition of the rusticated keystone, which causes the central area to expand. It is understandable how, faced with such an erudite but original and contrasting use of the classical language, Pietro Aretino expresses a double oxymoron when he praises Giulio's, "classically modern and modernly classical concepts". It was in this courtyard, then with its decoration incomplete, that Charles V was received, on April 2nd 1530. The emperor, thirty years old, like Federico Gonzaga, dismounted from "a beautiful female mule all embellished with gold and silk with all

Courtyard
of Honour,
north façade

30

Courtyard of Honour, east façade. Detail of the frieze with the slipped down tryglyph

his guards on parade, with all the Princes, Lords and Gentlemen and with the Marquis at his side", to start a day of pleasure at the palazzo of "honest leisure".

Loggia of the Muses

From the large square courtyard, Charles V moved on to the loggia of the Muses to enter the room of the Horses. The vestibule played an important role, not only as a spatial junction between one apartment and another and between interior and exterior, but also as a first approach, through its painting and sculpture, to the real reasons of the patron. Here, Federico Gonzaga wanted the visitor to be greeted with a show of the foremost cultural models of the ancient world. In the west lunette is a fresco of Apollo next to the winged horse Pegasus who, with a kick from his hoof, caused the spring of Hippocrene, dear to the muses, to flow on mount Helicon. The vault, with its low-relief decorations in highly ornate coffers, is dedicated to the goddesses of the arts and sciences. Around the pictures of the muses are painted panels with hieroglyphics: it is a homage to Egyptian civilisation, the language of which, according to long-standing tradition, was given directly by God to the descendents of Adam. During the Renaissance the language considered of divine origin was the perfect reference point for the creation of the "devices". We know that Giulio Romano, the only artist to do so in the sixteenth century, faithfully transcribed the mysterious hieroglyphics taken from two sphinxes that are nowadays at the Louvre. Given these divine origins, a celebration of Latin poetry could not be lacking. This was provided by its greatest exponent, Virgil, honoured as a poet in his native city of Mantua. Referred to him is the image we see painted in the east lunette: a wreathed head that emerges from the basin of a fountain from which water gushes. The same image depicted on coins, prints and paintings of the sixteenth century shows how it is a symbolic picture of Virgil, perhaps shown as a source of poetry and knowledge. A female figure is leaning on it, surrounded by symbols of knowledge, and in the background appears a cloaked no-

31

ble figure: the young girl is the personification of Mantua, united with her Virgil and watched over from above by a portrait of Apollo, inspired by the famous belvedere sculpture in the Vatican. On the walls are two badly damaged episodes from the myth of Orpheus and Eurydice, alluding to the victory of poetry over death and taken from Virgil's *Georgics* and Ovid's *Metamorphoses*. Among the many other purposes, the smiling putti on the doors next to the Gonzaga shield introduce a note of mischievousness as they bridle the bellicose Gonzaga eagles, in a foretaste of more entertaining topics.

Hall of the Horses

This is the only room in the palazzo that in structure and function is defined as a hall. It is larger and it marks the start of the more important

Loggia of the Muses.
West wall

route assigned to greeting guests and holding the chief events. Here too Giulio Romano shows off his classical knowledge, painting the walls with majestic architecture broken up by twin fluted Corinthian pilasters with rope-like motif in the lower part and embellished with highly coloured marble encrustation. Statues of divinities are housed in the wall alcoves and above the windows are busts of dignitaries; in the upper part of the bays imitation bronze low-reliefs given a reddish patina illustrate the labours of Hercules. But what immediately attracts the attention, in contrast to the clever and complex setting, are the life-size portraits of the horses painted in the lower parts of the bays. They appear to be outside the pilasters in a trompe l'oeil effect that brings them into our living space, as if they had leapt from the age of Giulio and Federico into the present. They look into the distance, their gazes filled with the excitement of races won, or turn toward us with the wild

33

eyes of the gentle steed. Like his father and his forefathers, Federico bred them in the famous Gonzaga stables, where they were loved and set great store by: a horse was the greatest gift he could give to a trusted friend like Giulio, or a great ruler like the emperor. The Palazzo Te horses stand out against a background of villages shown in perspective and their proportions, noble bearing and the interplay of light imparted by the range of different colours of their hide are all painted with masterly skill. The names of four of them are still known; from the right of the fireplace: Morel Favorito, Glorioso, Bataglia, Dario. The first and fourth still have their name written below. Even the Istrian stone fireplace is unusual, with certain parts given an almost complete finish, such as the jambs and architrave cornice, in striking contrast with the powerful rustication of the lintel. Another original interpretation of the classical repertoire is the frieze that runs around the top of the walls, incorporating the four Gonzaga eagles in the corners. The repeated, beautiful, multicoloured volutes are populated with playing male and female putti that cavort above threatening masks. The well-conserved ceiling, punctuated by a geometric interlay of plaited bands, has coffers containing rosettes and the devices of Olympus and the salamander in gilded wood on a blue background. Not a single name is to be found among the records to connect any artists to this ingenious room, probably executed between 1526 and 1528.

Once Charles V had dismounted in the courtyard of Honour and passed under the loggia of the Muses, he was received in this "beautiful large hall, where he stayed some time to look". Later, standing

34

Hall of the Horses
Ceiling, device
of the Olympos

on the side opposite the entrance, the sovereign was paid homage by
the other guests invited to the ball: gentlemen "and Gentlewomen of
the first order and beauty are to be found in Mantua". The celebrations ended late in the night, "in a flash over a thousand torches were
lit from every side, so that it seemed night had been turned into day";
when the king had been escorted to his lodgings in the Castle, "all
the Lords and Ladies were accompanied home [with the brightly lit
procession], and in this way the wonderful festivities held at palazzo
del Te were finished".

Chamber of Psyche

The "camaron quadro", square room, as it was called in an important sixteenth century description by Iacopo Strada, is the most sump-
tuous room in the villa. Its wealth of decoration is due partly to the
variety of topics covered, but also to the different techniques and
materials used. The frescoed walls with tempera finish are enclosed
by moulded stucco frames; the wooden vault covered with a fine layer of intonaco is divided into compartments painted in oils and
framed by gilded stucco work. The name of the room comes from
Apuleius's story of Amor and Psyche in his *Metamorphoses*. The Latin
writer adds the tale as a digression from his long novel, also known
as *The Golden Ass*. The twenty-two extracts illustrated by Giulio Romano are briefly summarised here to explain the meaning of one of
the Te's most famous painted cycles. 1- In a faraway city a king and
queen have three daughters, all beautiful, but the beauty of Psyche
far exceeds that of the others, to the point that she is rendered homage
and sacrifices are made to her as a mark of devotion; 2- Venus, an-
gry about this sacrilege tells Amor to punish Psyche by shooting her
with a dart that will make her fall in love with the most abject of
creatures; 3- As Amor is arming his infallible bow he pierces himself with his own arrow while looking at Psyche, with whom he falls
instantly in love; 4- The sisters marry but no one asks for Psyche's
hand. Apollo's oracle is consulted and it reveals that Psyche will marry a being not human, wicked and feared even by the gods; 5- The
princess left alone, as instructed by the oracle, on the top of a mountain is picked up and taken far away by Zephyr. The image of Neptune refers to the winds, which correspond to the will of the god;
6- Psyche, set down among the grass and flowers of a distant valley,
falls asleep exhausted; 7- When she awakens she finds before her a
magnificent palace. The doors open before her and she is given a
banquet by invisible beings; 8- From that moment on Psyche lives
happily in the palace where every night a mysterious and tender lover

comes to visit, who does not want to be seen by her. But her sisters, who go to visit her and are jealous of the wealth and happiness, persuade her that the night-time visitor is none other than the monster announced by the oracle. They suggest she gets up during the night and kills the monster living next to her. The octagon contains the moment in which Psyche greets her sisters, giving them clothes and jewels; 9- Psyche is convinced by her sisters and follows their advice, but when she sees her mysterious husband—the god Amor in person, she is enchanted and, filled with emotion, her trembling hand spills drops of boiling oil from her lamp on to the breast of Amor. He wakes up and, crying out in pain, flees from Psyche. *The story continues in the lunettes.* 10- Venus, who hears the cries of Amor and discovers she has been betrayed, calls her son, reprimands and threatens him; 11- Ceres and Juno intervene on Amor's behalf; 12- The fleeing Psyche asks Ceres for help, but she is rejected; 13- Now desperate, she begs the help of Juno in vain; 14- Venus climbs mount Olympus and asks Jupiter for Mercury's help in finding the fugitive; 15- Mercury, messenger of the gods, sends out orders to capture Psyche; 16- Psyche is captured by Habit, who drags her by the hair, while Restlessness and Sadness start to torture her on the orders of Venus; 17- Psyche is forced to undergo dangerous and arduous trials. The first involves sorting seeds from a huge pile and she succeeds thanks to the help of compassionate ants; 18- In the second, Psyche has reached a flock of sheep with golden fleece, climbing mountains and wading a river, which appears oddly personified in the fresco. The animals are ferocious and the desperate Psyche is about to throw herself off a cliff, but a reed (personified on the right) tells her to wait: once the heat of the day has passed, the sheep calm down and Psyche manages to gather the gold tufts of wool entangled among the thorns that Venus has demanded; 19- In the third trial, Psyche draws water from the infernal river Styx, guarded by terrible dragons. She succeeds only because Jupiter, who is starting to feel sorry for her, sends his eagle to help her ; 20- Fourth trial. Psyche reaches the underworld, cleverly overcoming all the dangers and traps on the way, to end up in the presence of queen Proserpine (Persephone) and ask humbly for a little of her beauty to bring back to Venus in a jar. The queen of the underworld agrees, but lays down one rule: Psyche must not open the jar; 21- Psyche, once back in the sunlight, cannot restrain her curiosity and takes the lid off the jar. An ethereal poison escapes and she falls to the ground, dying. At this point Amor, cured and overcome by longing, hastens to awaken Psyche and restore her health with a touch from one of

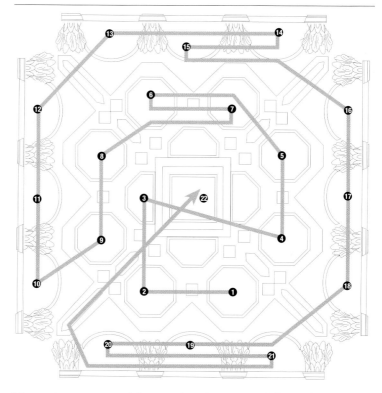

his magic arrows; 22- The panel in the centre of the vault shows the apotheosis of Amor and Psyche. Jupiter welcomes the princess on mount Olympus and, giving her the gift of immortality, marries her to Amor.

On the south and west walls are the preparations for a banquet attended by the gods. Present too are Amor and Psyche, lying on the *klíne*, the bed used at table by the ancients. On the espalier is the *ouroboros*, the snake that bites its own tail as a symbol of eternity, and between the bride and bridegroom their daughter Pleasure is already present. This detail leads Verheyen to reject the idea that this is the wedding banquet after the apotheosis, since Pleasure was not born by then. Verheyen considers the fresco to refer to the description of a banquet that takes place on the island of Venus, described in the *Hypnerotomachia Poliphili* (*The dream of Poliphilo*), a story written in 1499 and one of the most beautifully illustrated books ever published. Wherever we look, we see borders of water and we seem personally to attend the banquet from the centre of the island of Venus; perhaps we are also being invited to identify the island of the Te. On the north wall to the left of the window is *Mars and Venus bathing*, and to the

right *Venus preventing Mars from chasing Adonis.* Both episodes appear in the Renaissance text, as does the detail that Venus in the second episode treads by mistake on a rose: her divine blood is tinged with red and the miracle repeats itself every year to commemorate the anniversary of the death of Adonis. In the panel above the window *Bacchus and Ariadne* embrace on the island of Naxos. In the centre of the fireplace wall is a huge painting of *Polyphemus with Galatea and Acis*: despite his brutality the one-eyed giant is touched by love. His heart throbs for Galatea (who, in love with Acis, ignores him), and to win her over he plays music on his rustic bagpipe and brings her the small bear seen to the left. Above the left-hand side window an amorous meeting is taking place between *Jupiter and Olympia*. The king of the gods, victim of the arrows of Amor, turns himself into a snake to unite himself with the queen of Macedonia: the union produces Alexander the Great. King Phillip, who dares to enter the nuptial bed, is blinded by a thunderbolt hurled by Jupiter's eagle. Jupiter has been said to represent Federico Gonzaga, whose name appears deliberately above the panel in the frame containing the dedication. After all, Federico loved Isabella Boschetti, a young married woman. In the right–hand side panel, to stress the blind tyranny of Amor the moment is shown when Pasiphae, queen of Crete, gets inside the ar-

40

tificial cow that Daedalus has made to help her approach the bull with whom she has fallen in love. This unnatural union leads to the birth of the Minotaur. Neo-Platonism is often used to explain the meaning of this complicated decorative cycle: from the extravagant dominion of the senses, the final moment of purification and apotheosis of the soul are reached. More likely, instead, is a hedonistic interpretation, which sees Amor as a tyrant, feared by the gods and more powerful than Jupiter himself (not forgetting the prophesy that Psyche would marry an evil being), and forcing everyone to obey his commands. And like mankind and the gods of the myth, Federico is forced to obey Amor, victim of his arrows. The idea that the story of Amor and Psyche alludes to Federico's personal situation does not appear unfounded: his relationship with his *favorita* Isabella Boschetti was opposed by his mother Isabella, who takes on the role of the resentful Venus. Vasari writes that the frescoes, significantly retouched by Giulio, can be considered largely autograph works. In truth, the quality of the conception is high, while the level of execution is discontinuous. The finest parts are generally considered to be: the dresser, with its sparkling silver and glass on the southern wall, and the gods that surround it; the left-hand side of the adjoining wall with its beautiful

Chamber of Amor and Psyche. East wall

On the following pages Chamber of Amor and Psyche. South wall

41

ET·REIP·FLOR· CAPI

NEVS· GENERALIS·

HONESTO·OCIO   POST·LABORES   AD·REPARANDAM

landscape of nymphs and river gods; Mars and Venus bathing; Polyphemus and scenes from the story by Apuleius, among which: Psyche and the source of the Styx, Venus chasing away Amor, Psyche and Proserpine. We know from records that also working on the frescoes were Giovan Francesco Penni and Rinaldo Mantovano, to whom Benedetto Pagni da Pescia can be added. The large red Verona marble fireplace with stucco hood decorated with a band of plant shoots, reads: F<edericus> GONZAGA II M<archio> M<antuae> V S<anctae> R<omanae> E<cclesiae> C<apitaneus> G<eneralis>: Federico II Gonzaga Fifth Marquis of Mantua Captain General of the Holy Roman Church. The dedication for the palazzo as a whole appears on the cornice running along the bottom of the lunette: FEDERICVS GONZAGA II MAR<chio> V S<anctae> R<omanae> E<cclesiae> ET REIP<ublicae> FLOR<entinae> CAPITANEVS GENERALIS HONESTO OCIO POST LABORES AD REPARANDAM VIRT<utem> QUIETI CONSTRVI MANDAVIT: Federico II Gonzaga Fifth Marquis Captain General of the Holy Roman Church and of the Florentine Republic ordered its construction for his honest leisure after hard work to regain his strength in peace.

This room marks the beginning of a sequence of beautifully designed and carefully crafted floors in Venetian style "terrazzo" mosaic, executed between 1784 and 1786 from drawings by the architect Paolo

Chamber of Amor and Psyche. West wall

Pozzo. The floors, in the six rooms in the east wing, are particularly precious due to the background colour made up of marble tesserae and the coloured mortar used to connect the pieces.

Charles V showed his preference for this exceptional room: "We went into the *Camarone,* and on seeing it his Majesty was utterly amazed, and he stayed there over half an hour in contemplation, praising each thing highly". He ate dinner here: "His majesty returned to dine, and ate in the large *Camarone* on the left-hand side near the window that overlooks the garden; and our Illustrious Signor Marchese that morning served him by giving his Majesty the cloth with which to dry his hands".

Chamber of the Winds

The name derives from the faces with puffed out cheeks that personify the winds and blow from the groin above the lunettes. The main subject is linked to texts about ancient astrological doctrine (Manilio and Firmico Materno): in the vault the twelve signs of the zodiac are depicted as stucco low-reliefs made to look like bronze. Under each sign a frescoed medallion shows the skills or activities induced by one of the three constellations that are subjected to that sign. Some of the signs, as we shall see, have two medallions. How mankind's destiny depends on the stars is also repeated in the writing on the architrave of the south door, taken from a satire by Giovenal: DISTAT ENIM QVAE SIDERA TE EXCIPIANT: it depends precisely on which stars greet you (at birth). At the top of the vault, three panels with the devices of Olympus, Vulcan and Vesta are set in the middle of interconnected octagons divided into ten elongated hexagons that contain frescoes of ten deities. Starting from the hexagon beneath the feet of Vulcan, we see Juno; continuing in the direction of his chariot pulled by peacocks, we come to: Neptune, Minerva, Venus, Apollo, Mercury, Jupiter, Ceres; in the central hexagons: Mars and Diana. In the outer strip, alternating with the imitation bronze signs of the zodiac are painted personifications and allegories of the months. From the first hexagon under Juno's chariot: January, with the picture of Janus; February, with Faunus, to whom the *Lupercalia* celebrations were dedicated; March, with the god Mars; April, with the birth of Venus, traditionally set in this month; May: Maya, to whom the month is dedicated, with her son Mercury; June: Juno; July: Julius Caesar, from whom the name for the month traditionally derives; August: Augustus; September: an unidentified Roman emperor; October: an unidentified Roman emperor; November; the transplanting of a tree trunk; December: the olive harvest. The medallions at the top of the walls start with the first sign of the year, illustrated at the beginning of the *south wall*, to the left of the fireplace: Capricorn (21 December–19 January), constellation of the Serpentarium: the snake charmer; Aquarius (20 January–18 February): the victorious general; Pisces (19 February–20 March), constellation of the Whale: fishermen of large fish in the abysses; Aries (21 March–20 April), constellation of the Ship and Dolphin: navigators. The Auriga constellation is also connected to the same sign: music of shepherds. *West wall*: Taurus (21 April–20 May), Pleiades, ascendant Bull's Hoof: gladiators; Gemini (21 May–21 June), constellation of the Hare: fast runners, with the story of the myth of Atalanta and Hippomenes; Cancer (21 June–22 July), constellation of Orion: hunters. On the *north wall* is a second medallion referring to the constellation, with fishermen; Leo (23 July–22 August) constellation of the dog: hunters of huge wild beasts; Virgo (23 August–23 September), constellation of the Crown: a collection of perfumed essences and garlands; Libra (23 September–22 October), constellation of the arrow: hunters with bows; Scorpio (23 October–21 November), constellation of the Altar: priests. The same constellation, as illustrated in the first medallion on the *east wall*, favours the profession of the charioteer; Sagittarius (22 November–20 December), constellation of Arthur on the wane: criminals in prison; in the same sign, but with Arthur on the rise: guardians of the homes of sovereigns.

Work was going on in the room between September 1527 and August 1528. Sculptor Nicolò da Milano was paid for the stucco figures and festoons, while stuccoist Andrea di Pezi was paid for the acanthus leaves on the corbels and for all the framing work, which was moulded. Working on the painted parts were Anselmo Guazzi (10 hexagons), Agostino da Mozzanica (2), Benedetto Pagni (1) and Gerolamo da Treviso (9). Gerolamo's contribution has been rightly identified (Carpi, Mancini) in the central hexagons representing: Neptune, Minerva, Apollo and Mars, and in the outer ones with Janus, Juno, Julius Caesar, Emperor with Victory, the olive harvest. To the hand of the mediocre Agostino we can assign the hexagon with Mars-March and the Transplant-November, and attribution is agreed to Pagni for the Faun of the Lupercalia, as suggested by Oberhuber. Anselmo Guazzi, who loved soft, elongated shapes, delicate tones and pinkish complexions is responsible for the other ten lozenges. There is no known documentation about the medallions in the frieze; Mancini recognises, probably rightly, the hand of Gerolamo in the first four (Capricorn, Aquarius, Pisces, Whale). Oberhuber's suggestion that

Chamber
of the Winds.
Constellation of the
Ship and Dolphin.
Navigators

Giulio Romano himself was responsible for the medallion of the Lion is plausible in view of the quality which distinguishes it. However, the high quality of all the medallions can be admired, and there are other finely painted examples: the *Gladiators* of Taurus, the *Hunters* and *Fishermen* of Cancer, the *Sacrifice* of Scorpio. In the parts that cannot be attributed to Gerolamo, Pagni is likely to have played a fundamental part. The fireplace is made of Brentonico marble, as are the door frames in this room and the previous one, chosen for its variegated colour. In the centre of the fireplace hood is a black and white Aquitaine marble disc surrounded by volutes with pairs of putti and salamanders. The inscription is carved on the architrave: F<edericus> G<onzaga> II M<archio> M<antuae> V S<anctis>S<imae> R<omanae> E<cclesiae> C<apitaneus> G<eneralis>: Federico II Gonzaga Fifth Marquis of Mantua Captain General of the Holy Roman Church. The decoration and its creator were admired by Charles V: "His majesty withdrew into the chamber of the winds and spoke for an hour publicly with Cardinal Cibo, praising this room greatly, and also the Maestro and inventor of it and of its so many diversities, and in detail did His Majesty wish to understand everything".

Chamber of the Eagles

Also known as the chamber of Phaeton due to the subject in the central octagon, this is the smallest of the decorated rooms in the east wing and it was used by Federico Gonzaga as his bed chamber. The decoration is some of the most complex and highly detailed, with painting and relief work in constant alternation. It has the finest marbles and was once largely decorated in fine gold leaf. The name derives from the four large black eagles that stretch out their wings from large gilded alcoves. The central octagon contains the *Fall of Phaeton*. He was the son of Apollo and he had dared to drive the sun chariot but was unable to keep it on course, producing such damage to the earth that Jupiter was forced to stop it with a thunderbolt. This myth is generally understood as a warning not to overstep the mark, but in Verheyen's opinion it may allude to the greatness of Mantua's historic past: Phaeton fell into the Po and it was from the region through which the river passed that the rebirth of the world took place, the golden age. In the vault the quadripartite decoration, framed by vine shoots inhabited by lively putti playing, running, jumping and performing somersaults is the work of Primaticcio, as shown by a document dated 1527 and by the high quality of the work. Also attributed to the great Bolognese painter are the four panels surrounding the central octagon showing: *Neptune abducting Amphitrite*; *Jupiter, now transformed into a bull, abducting Europa*; *Mercury before Jupiter, Juno and Neptune*; *Pluto abducting Proserpine*. The elegance of the drapery, the harmony of the bodies and the pulsating vitality of the animals are striking. Four lunettes divided into panels which echo a similar scheme at Villa Madama, are decorated with stucco work on the outer bands and partitions and seem to rest on the corbels embellished with high relief harpies. In the stucco roundels of the bands are delicate compositions with putti very similar to those in the vine shoots; these "cameos" can as a result also be ascribed to Primaticcio, who directed the decoration work. Nicolò da Milano is recorded in a payment for four caryatids in the centre of the lunette, for two of the ovals projecting from the corners and for one of the trophies in the frieze. It is also likely that he executed the other two ovals and the remaining trophies; for stylistic reasons

Chamber of the Eagles. Firewall, detail of the cowl

he can also be held responsible for the harpies energetically jutting
out from the corbels. Andrea di Pezi was paid for the leaf decorations
in the lunettes and for the two masks at the top of them. The six panels in each lunette are painted with mythological figures, although the
subjects do not appear connected. The only date available on the painted decoration concerns the payment for four days' work to Agostino
da Mozzanica, recorded in July 1528. Of very high level are instead
the four bands painted at the base of the lunettes which represent,
starting from the window to the right: a *Battle between Animals and
Monsters*; *Battle among Sea Monsters*; *Fighting between the Greeks and*

Amazons; Centaurmachia. Primaticcio also may have contributed to these battles, turbulent and dynamic in composition, original and elegant in detail; there is no proof, however. The fireplace is made from "lumachella" marble from the Trento foothills and its fine colours range from wine red to deep earth green; the furrowed hood, with the salamanders at the edges shifting towards the fire, was once covered in fine gold. Of even greater value are the door frames in Greek "portasanta" marble, the same material was used for the Porta Santa at St Peter's basilica in Rome in 1525. These portals, like those at St Peter's, were executed in the same year by the same marble carver, but the pieces for Palazzo Te were only delivered after a long time. Brought by sea from Civitavecchia to Venice, and then to Mantua, they did not arrive until October 1526.

The Holy Roman Emperor particularly admired the rare marble in this room: "Then [the Emperor] entered the other room, called Chamber of the Eagles, which is magnificent with two superb doors of oriental jasper for this room, and a table also of jasper, about which his Majesty had a great deal to say, with the place where the fire burns made of very fine variegated marble". The writing on the architrave commemorates the patron: F<edericus> II G<onzaga> M<archio> M<antuae> V: Federico second Gonzaga fifth marquis of Mantua. Because Charles V made Federico a duke when he visited Mantua in April 1530, all the inscriptions bearing his title as marquis can be safely dated earlier than this.

Loggia of David

The huge loggia, as big as the hall of the Horses, comes as a surprise to visitors whether they come from the chamber of the Eagles or through the portal of the courtyard of Honour. It has a vast barrel vault and a triple arch supported in the centre by unusual tetrastyle columns, and at the sides columns and double pillars. The solemn and luminous architecture enhances the view of the garden which extends beyond the arches and was once luxuriant with plants and flowers. The iconography of this space is dedicated to a Biblical character rather than a mythological hero. But David is depicted as a valiant young man overcoming a lion and a bear, defeating the giant Goliath and also showing his gifts as a great poet and musician by composing psalms. However, he falls in love with Bathsheba, whom he sees as she is bathing and, unable to bear the fact that she is married, sends her husband Uriah to die in battle after getting him drunk (south octagon). Like David, Federico could not stand to share his *favorita* with her husband, Francesco di Calvisano, and, after accusing him of a plot hired a killer to murder him. The other ideals of good government introduced by the tributes to David's accomplishments serve by their specious interpretation of the precedent in the Bible to legitimise his adultery and the murder he committed. The loggia, probably already built in time for the Charles V celebrations in 1530, was given temporary decoration in 1532 on the occasion of the sovereign's second visit. The current decoration was carried out between 1532 and 1534 and was some of the most recent work done at the palazzo. Luca da Faenza carried out the three west lunettes: the centre, a Gonzaga shield surmounted by the Olympus bestowed by the emperor, surrounded by putti; to the left *David fighting the bear*, to the right *David fighting the lion*. The top lunette with *David and Goliath* is by Rinaldo Mantovano; the one opposite, with David playing the lyre, by Fermo da Caravaggio. The *Toilette* and *Bathsheba bathing* are by Rinaldo and *The drunkenness of Uriah* by Benedetto Pagni. Pagni was also paid for six of the eight putti which alternate with the arches, and for five of

Loggia of David

52

Loggia of David,
*The Toilette
of Betsabea*

*On the following
pages*
Loggia of David

the eight masks sneering above the putti. The moulding, richly ornate and of fine quality, is partly sixteenth century, the cornice and vault, and part of the walls, second half of the eighteenth century. The ornate oval cornices, palmettes and other classical motifs are moulded by brothers Andrea and Biagio de Conti, with Benedetto di Bertoldo responsible for the floral friezes with gryphons in the central octagons. Two noteworthy cycles are modelled by one sculptor: the twelve figures (Victories, mythological and allegorical characters) in the pendentives of the arches, and the ten medallions, with episodes from the *Stories of David* which decorate the lunettes at either end. The former are modelled with a more marked relief, while that of the roundels is less accentuated. However, the two groups share stylistic affinities: bodies with solid anatomy, broad drapery and wide light surfaces, but also a certain difficulty in fitting in with Giulio's complex organisation of space. The manner is that of Giovan Battista Mantovano, the only sculptor continuing in the tradition of Nicolò da Milano and Primaticcio who was by then no longer on the site. Federico Gonzaga wanted the alcoves (smaller than they are now) to contain marble busts of famous military leaders, and had commissioned Alfonso Cittadella to sculpt them, but due to various problems the project was not carried out. The present fourteen statues in gallina stone of the *Virtues,* largely inspired by Ripa's *Iconology*, were placed here in 1653 and are probably the work of Bolognese sculptor, Gabriele Brunelli. The poorly conserved imitation bronze low-reliefs on the walls, which continue on the Biblical theme of the stories of David are by Veronese Giovanni Bellavite, professor at the Academy of Mantua, and were carried out between 1808 and 1809.

Charles V, escorted from the loggia to the entrance to the garden, was entertained by the acrobatics of two splendid Gonzaga horses, "with the finest trappings one can imagine, with deep blue velvet ornamentation and a harness of full and cut out patterns, fringes of velvet embroidered in gold everywhere, with their bows of gold deep blue silk, they were a magnificent sight; they were made to move in the garden before his Majesty who stood to watch them (go) to the garden entrance, where the bridge lies, finely arrayed with obstacles as

tall as the horses. And the aforesaid Signor Marchese gave these horses as a gift to his Majesty, accompanying with it the words best suited to the gift and to his Majesty, who greatly praised the horses and thanked him profusely".

Chamber of the Stuccoes

Once past the loggia, one enters the Chamber of the Stuccoes: decorated solely with relief work of the highest level, it is one of the most pleasant rooms in the villa. It is the Italian masterpiece of Francesco Primaticcio, carried out with Giovan Battista Mantovano on the eve of Francesco's departure for the French court, probably between 1529 and 1531. Giorgio Vasari, who met Primaticcio in Bologna in 1563 and therefore had news straight "from the horse's mouth", ascribes the work to these two artists, one Bolognese and the other Mantuan. A close look at these magnificent stuccoes confirms the attribution, despite recent doubts by several experts. The barrel vault is divided into twenty-five panels, low-relief work sculpted on a black background, as finely carved as cameos made of semi-precious stones in the delicacy of the modelling and clarity of outline. They represent characters from mythology and classical history, with the unexplained exception of a scene of an ancient *Baptism*; some of the scenes are modelled with the elegance, naturalness and liveliness we observed previously in Primaticcio's work in the chamber of the Eagles. The others, on the other hand, less expertly crafted with less successfully drawn anatomies and facial expressions, can be attributed to Mantovano. There are also intermediate levels of quality, which lead one to suppose that the two sculptors worked closely together. Among the finest "cameos" are: *Mercury, Venus and Amor, Neptune, Gladiators, The reawakening of Ariadne, Jupiter and the three Virtues, Silenus and Fortune*. The lunettes are filled with simulated marble alcoves containing life-size high relief figures of Hercules and Mars. These sculptures too are worthy of attribution to Primaticcio, while the *Victories* crowning the lunettes are probably by Giovan Battista. Along the walls below runs a double frieze depicting "la milizia antica de' romani", or rather the varied composition of a Roman army on the march. The sequence starts in the left corner of the wall opposite the entrance, upper band: we see the rear guard coming out of a city gate with the carts carrying provisions and the farewell salutes to the families of the soldiers; marching on the right are the slingsmen preceded on the adjoining wall by soldiers with lances. Further on, a number of standard bearers and other soldiers armed with gladius and shield (among whom a child wearing a helmet) are amassing at a ford. At the beginning of the next,

Chamber of the
Stuccoes. Detail
of the double frieze

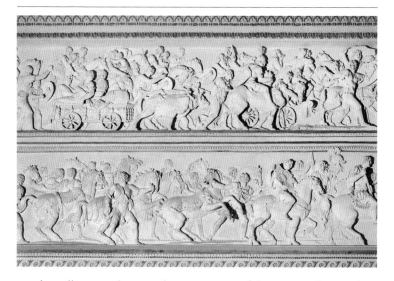

north, wall we see the complex operations of the men as they undress
and cross the river with effort and taking great care, holding their bun-
dles up on their shields. The march proceeds orderly and the next river, personified on the right-hand side of the wall, is crossed thanks to
a bridge with a strong parapet. On the window wall, archers and lancers
on horseback group into squads or spread out in a fast gallop. Following on in the lower band of the south wall, we see the cavalcade
continue and then gradually stop because the horsemen have dismounted and are holding their chafing horses by the bit: nearby, the
emperor advances on horseback with his hand held out, issuing orders. Behind him, an equerry holds up a two-headed eagle, an anachro-
nistic tribute to the Hapsburg sovereign. Preceding the emperor are
the lictors and musicians with a fine array of instruments; further ahead,
on the west wall, augurs and haruspexes are busy talking, while priests
and animal sacrificers carry with them the animals to be killed. In the
centre is a graphic detail of a horse urinating, while a little further on
a young man shows off another modern shield with the Gonzaga emblem (datable before 1530), a homage to the patron and his presumed
military triumphs. The band continues on the north wall with horsemen fording a river, exactly opposite the ford illustrated in the upper
frieze: the generous efforts of the horses are compared with the en-
deavours of the men on foot. Further on, an armourer with his cart
loaded with equipment and weapons, a carpenter and other artisans
precede the body of the troops to set up camp and organise the fa-
cilities. They are travelling with eastern slaves who with their pack-
saddle horses, camels and mules transport the vanguard supplies. The

route back up of the ranks we have followed ends on the window wall, where two squadrons of horsemen are launched at a gallop: the first wears scale armour, like that of the Sarmates; the second, on the other side of the window, is armed in Roman style and its men are wielding iron clubs.

Clearly Giulio's most important iconographical precedents were the columns of Trajan and Marcus Aurelius, although none of the figures from them have been copied in this composition. The frieze is over sixty metres long and contains some five hundred figures of women, men, youths and animals. One can imagine the artist ideally comparing his work with Mantegna's *Triumphs*, in the great painter's ability to bring to life a historic procession of soldiers with exceptional truthfulness and enormous knowledge of classical times. The stucco work taken from ideas by Giulio are still the focus of a discussion about authorship. Recently, critics have supported Vasari's claim that the work was by Primaticcio and Giovan Battista Mantovano, who worked side by side. It has not been decided as yet who was responsible for what, however. Mantovano's modelling seems more rapid and deliberately sketchy in his definition of the physiognomies, which remain as if roughly defined in soft matter, with facial expressions that are almost caricatures. Primaticcio, instead, seems to model like the classical sculptors, or like the magnificent low-relief work by Antonio Lombardo in the Alfonso d'Este chamber of Alabaster. Aiming at formal perfection and courtly pronouncement, it is distinct from the affable, almost common and vaguely sketched manner of Giovan Battista. By Primaticcio are the more plastically accentuated reliefs in the bands on the wall opposite the entrance, in particular the section with the emperor and his retinue. The proud virile heads are modelled and smoothed to look like classical marble, and show heroic traits; the same is true for the beautiful horses: with their nervous and twitchy gait, they stretch out their quivering heads, displaying a flash of muscle, dilated nostrils and the blood coursing through their veins. This is far removed from the humorous and complacent description of the crowd of soothsayers on the west wall, where the dilated figures are modelled in lower relief, the details of the face set with quick fingerprint marks! The solid relief by Primaticcio continues in the upper frieze on the other walls and in the right-hand side half of the lower east-side frieze beside the window; the other walls seem to be the work of Mantovano, who with this composition reaches his peak as a sculptor.

Chamber of the Emperors

Continuing in this room, also known as the chamber of Caesar, is iconography linked to the ancient world, bearers of *exempla virtutis* befitting decorations for a Renaissance prince. In the centre of the vault is a large panel showing *Caesar Ordering Pompeius' Letters to be Burnt* after the victory of Pharsalus: he does not want to know the schemes that linked his beaten enemy to the notables of Rome. The episode is successfully illustrated, the figures are elegant and the colour tones are light and lively, which makes the traditional attribution to Primaticcio feasible—accepted what is more by Dimier, the artist's biographer. Today there is more caution, in the absence of proven documentation regarding the Bolognese painter's work in Mantua or specific archive references; it should be added that the drawings by Giulio that Primaticcio took to Paris probably includ-

ed the one regarding the scene in question, now in the Louvre. The
vault contains six vertical rectangles, one on the short sides and two
on the long ones, separated by a roundel. The rectangles illustrate
figures of emperors and warriors; starting from the one near the window and continuing to the right are: *Alexander the Great, Julius Caesar*; a warrior with a lion's skin; *Augustus*; warrior; *Philip of Macedonia*. The roundel next to Caesar provides an example of mag-
nanimousness by Alexander the Great. After the victory at Gaza, the
soldiers brought Alexander a magnificent casket, the object of greatest value found among the spoils, and Alexander, the Macedon says
he will put his most prized possessions in it, and places there the
Iliad and the *Odyssey*. In the roundel on the opposite side is the *Con-
tinence of Scipio*. The episode describes how the Roman condottiere
returns a young woman given him as a slave after a victory to her
betrothed, the prince of the defeated Celtiberes. In Oberhuber's opinion *Augustus*, the four personages near the roundel and the *Conti-
nence of Scipio* are the work of Rinaldo Mantovano; the scholar attributes to Giulio himself the panel with Alexander the Great and
the roundel with the scene of the sovereign and the books by Homer.

In the corners, a victory and two putti in stucco hold four of the Gonzaga devices: the small wood (boschetto), the salamander and the Olympus we have already seen, and the Zodiac. The Zodiac, complex astronomically and astrologically shows the earth immobile in the firmament. The motto states IN EODEM SEMPER (ever in the same place): a sign of faithfulness in love. The chronology of the decoration is under debate, but it seems reasonable to date it at the same time as the work in the adjoining room of the Stuccoes. The dating 1529–1530 allows the question of Primaticcio's contribution to remain open and attribution of the stuccoes to Nicolò da Milano for stylistic reasons that appear convincing: there are close affinities with these *Victories*, from the modelling at once vigorous, refined and sharply defined, with the works documented as being by his hand, in particular the *Victories* in the chamber of the same name, with the *Caryatids* in the chamber of the Winds, and with the *Harpies*, already attributed to him in the chamber of the Eagles. The band of putti and medallions in the frieze painted in chiaroscuro to look like relief work is by Mantuan painter Felice Campi. Executed in 1788–1789 during restoration work the Austrian government com-

Chamber
of the Emperors.
The vault

61

missioned the Accademia di Belle Arti to execute, it replaced an early XVIII century frieze which in turn replaced a lost original.

Chamber of the Giants

This is the most famous room in the villa, and the originality and expressive power of its images still manages to surprise visitors even today. It is the only room where there is no moulding and in which the architecture itself is denied and contradicted by the success of the painted figures. Vasari described the room in detail and was a good witness of the effect its creator was aiming for. Giulio received Vasari in Mantua in 1541 and "for four days never left him, showing him all his works". Giulio conceived the most daring experiment in the history of modern painting: he concealed the architectural boundaries of the room rounding off the sharp corners of the walls, and those between the walls and the vault, so that the painting had no spatial limits other than those of the figurative composition. Spectators enter a dimension that is complete and all-absorbing artistic invention, where they can experience the journey through space and time that has been established by the painter. Vasari also tells us that the floor was made up of a mosaic of river pebbles that continued at the base of the walls in the part now altered by eighteenth century restoration work. This meant that the interruption between horizontal and vertical planes was also eliminated and the observer was plunged straight into the invention. The artist, fully in command, brings to life the mythological tale of the *Fall of the Giants*, whom we see fighting and tumbling to the ground around us, drawing us wholly into the scene. The story tells how the Giants, wicked inhabitants of the earth, tried to scale mount Olympus and take the place of the gods. Unable to gain direct access to the holy mountain, they piled mount Ossa on top of mount Pelion to climb to the summit. But Jupiter, assisted by the other inhabitants of Olympus, hurled his thunderbolts and unleashed the elements against the huge mountain of the giants. It collapsed, knocking over the foolhardy and cruel assailants, who are still now buried under the immense boulders. The moment depicted is that of divine revenge, with the mountains collapsing and the giants either crushed by the rocks or trying a last ditch attempt to save themselves. The tumbling mountain merges with the ruined palaces so that the painted architecture, which replaces the real, also seems to be wrecked. There is hardly an element of calm, not even in the beautiful, dizzy-making and violently wind-blown landscapes. Only Jupiter's throne at the top of the unreachable sky remains divinely peaceful. The eye shifts from the gods, frightened or huddled together, to the

huge, crushed bodies and the monstrous giants trying to flee from the devastation and to the billowing winds that drifts towards us, the on-lookers. On the east wall, between the windows there was a fireplace, whose traces can still be seen. Above it Pluto hurries to Sicily, worried by the earthquakes taking place there: it is the fault of the giant Typheus, who, left buried under the rocks of the island, assumed a triangular shape pose and began to erupt fire and flames. The trick leads from the real flames in the fireplace to the ones that come out of the giant's mouth to the irrepressible eruption that is pouring forth from the peak of Etna, the island's volcano. Next to him and other giants, near the stream of blood flowing from the wounds, some monkeys can be seen. These are the result of a mistaken interpretation that appeared in some vernacular versions of Ovid's *Metamorphoses*, the chief source for this tale. The poet of Sulmo says "scires e sanguine natos": you should know that [the violent giants] were born from blood. The legend tells that they were born from the drops of blood poured by Uranus on to the earth: born under the sign of violence and condemned to it. But some translators mistakenly read: "simiae e sanguine natae": monkeys—a common symbol of baseness—were born from their blood (Guthmüller). Low down, between the entrance door and the window on the broken lintel of the arch is a passage written later (perhaps during the eighteenth century restoration work?) and taken from Statius: [QUAENAM SPES] HOMINUM TUMIDAE POST PRAELIA PHLEGRAE. It can be translated: "what are the hopes of man after the assaults by the rebel Flegra?" Flegra is the region in Macedonia, near Olympus, where the giants' rebellion reputedly began.

This spectacular piece of art can rightly be given a political meaning: it is a homage to the supreme power of the emperor, and it is clearly shown how Charles V is in the guise of Jupiter striking down the giants symbolically depicted in a celebratory medallion (Perina). A hidden meaning might also connect Jupiter's kingliness to the ambitious Federico, who had chosen mount Olympus as his own personal emblem to add to the family crest. In this room Giulio Romano expresses a powerful inventiveness which places him at the vanguard of figurative studies at the time. Raphael's lesson is still present in terms of the last of the Vatican Rooms, but it has evolved to include, in as much as possible, the powerful example of Michelangelo's vault in the Sistine chapel and, in the absurd attempt by the giants to flee from the rubble, one seems to see echoes of his *Prisoner* sculptures now at the Louvre, in Paris. The explosion of such energy, supported by the grandeur of the images, such incontrovertible "terribleness", despite its grotesqueness, anticipates

Michelangelo's dramatic composition *The Universal Judgement*. It
is surprising how Giulio manages to compose, within a short space
of time, cycles of measured and refined classicism, like the relief
work in the chamber of the Stuccoes, and the stage-like explosions
of energy seen here. Documents include payment certificates that
testify to the important role played by Rinaldo Mantovano in the
work begun in 1532 and still unfinished in 1534. He was probably responsible for the figures, while Luca da Faenza and Fermo
Ghisoni, minor assistants, were paid for having painted "landscapes
and mountains"; Fermo also painted half the "temple " of Jupiter
in the centre of the vault.

At eye level, all around the room is a series of writings, prevalently graffiti, masked but not eliminated during the restoration work of the 1990s. It records how the bad habit of leaving one's signature to mark one's presence in such a sublime place goes back a long way: the oldest dates belong to the sixteenth century; the lansquenets who sacked Mantua in the seventeenth century also left their autographs. The deplorable tradition, which persisted until the first half of the twentieth century, now seems to have stopped, partly thanks to CCTV cameras and custodians. The famous room, imitated by other painters and repeatedly reproduced in prints has not always appealed to its visitors, though. The harshest criticisms belong to the nineteenth century, when the ideals of beauty could hardly coincide with this Mannerist masterpiece. Some of the most uncommon remarks were made by Charles Dickens, who took a dislike to Mantua and its buildings and although intending to mock the room of the Giants, recorded better than anyone else the powerful impact of the frescoes: "there are dozens of Giants (Titans warring with Jove) on the walls of another room, so inconceivably ugly and grotesque, that it is marvellous how any man can have imagined such creatures. In the chamber in which they abound, these monsters, with swollen faces and cracked cheeks, and every kind of distortion of look and limb, are depicted as staggering under the weight of falling buildings, and being overwhelmed in the ruins; upheaving masses of rock, and burying themselves beneath; vainly striving to sustain the pillars of heavy roofs that topple down upon their heads; and, in a word, undergoing and doing every kind of mad and demoniacal destruction. The figures are immensely large, and exaggerated to the utmost pitch of uncouthness; the colouring is harsh and disagreeable; and the whole effect more like (I should imagine) a violent rush of blood to the head of the spectator, than any real picture set before him by the hand of an artist. This apoplectic performance was shown by a sickly-looking woman, whose appearance was referable, I dare say, to the bad air of the marshes".

Small Cross Vault Chamber

The sequence of monumental rooms ends with the chamber of the Giants, which overlook the fish ponds and are especially rich in decoration and meaning. Now we come to a double apartment that occupies the south wing of the villa and is set around a large central space, the south loggia. The rooms set around the square courtyard were restored in 1813. The walls in particular were given a simulated marble finish, while door frames were made in *marmorino* stucco relief

by Gerolamo Staffieri of Ticino. The first, smallish, room, for private use like the adjoining ones, has a simple cross vault graciously painted with grotesques by Gerolamo da Pontremoli in 1534. Dated a year earlier are the vault stuccoes moulded by Biagio de Conti and Benedetto di Bertoldo; Andrea Conti completed the work by hand-modelling the acanthus leaves in the corbels, but there is no mention of the creator of the masks below.

Small Chamber of Grotesques

Also known as the chamber of Eight Sides, this small room has moulded stucco frames by Andrea Conti (1533). Lively and attractive are the small panels with playing putti between the ribbing, like cameos on a red or black background, supported laterally by larger putti: they are probably the work of Giovan Battista Mantovano, although the rapid modelling seems at times to compromise the quality. The imaginative grotesques, with flowers, insects, birds, imaginary animals and small genre or mythological figures are painted by Luca da Faenza, whose name is recorded in documents alongside that of Gerolamo da Pontremoli, responsible in particular for the roundel with Amor painted under the window arch.

Small Chamber of Venus

This small room served to connect the *stufetta*, once accessible from a now walled-up staircase leading to the mezzanine floor. The stucco work in the vault (the mouldings by Andrea de Conti) is almost entirely lost, but the grotesques, lively and original in colour were finely executed by Gerolamo da Pontremoli, who received payment for this work in 1534. Four bands containing swords, shields and quivers close the composition alluding to the martial virtues of his lordship. In the centre is a rectangle with a deep gold background, decorated with symmetrical plant shoots inhabited on the long sides by brightly coloured but delicately shaded small birds. There are two multicoloured harpies on the short sides and flying cherubs offering objects for the toilette in the four corners: a feather and a brush, perfume bottles, a small towel, mirror, combs and a turban. The central rectangle with plant shoots, putti and masks on a red background bears a roundel with a fine image of Venus at the mirror, her clothes and blond tresses fluttering around her as she is assisted by Cupid. It is surprising how cleverly Gerolamo shifts from the lifelike complexions and gentle flight of the birds to the metamorphoses that cause the plant motifs to adapt to a perfect geometry, taking on the reflection and texture of shining metal.

Chamber of the Candelabra

The decoration on the walls and ceiling, with its original wooden coffers, is the work of Staffieri (1813). The frieze instead is by Giulio.
The relief work was modelled at the end of 1527 by Nicolò da Milano and Giovan Battista Mantovano. Nicolò executed one of the "stories" in the rectangles in the centre of the walls, while Mantovano
carried out the other three. Nicolò was the author of the seven roundels
and five candelabra and the rest is by Giovan Battista. Given the lim-
ited modelling, it is hard to distinguish the work of one from the
other: Belluzzi's suggestion that Nicolò executed the most elegant of
the "stories", the Bacchic Choir on the east wall, seems acceptable.
The Milanese artist is also probably creator of the fine prisoner fig
ures, shown standing or kneeling, against a background of weapons
trophies at the corners of the room: not mentioned in the records,
they seem modelled with an energy influenced by Michelangelo. The
painting, with floral motifs, small figures and masks can be attributed to Agostino da Mozzanica.

Chamber of the Caryatids

The name is not old since, as recently shown, the caryatids and three
rectangular panels that decorate the walls come from two rooms by
Giulio in palazzo Ducale, brought here during Staffieri's renovation
work. The panels represent three parts of the day: *Dawn*, on the en-

Chamber of the
Candelabra.
Detail of the frieze

trance wall, *Day* and *Night*. The attribution to Primaticcio found
in the old guide books can be rejected because at the time when the
caryatids were modelled on the walls in the Imperial room and the
parts of the day in the Marbles gallery, Primaticcio had already been
working for the French court for some time. In the frieze instead
roundels set inside garlands that were part of the original decoration still survive, alternating with neoclassical female figures. The
allegorical or mythological figures in the roundels appear to be the
work of Nicolò da Milano.

South Loggia

This large room was originally designed as a loggia and it was to serve
the same purpose at that of the Muses on the other side of the courtyard. In actual fact, by the second half of the sixteenth century the
vault was still not covered and it remained an unfinished space. The
present-day layout of the walls and wooden ceiling are the result of
restoration work planned by Paolo Pozzo in 1790. In the middle of
the room is a wooden model of Palazzo Te built for the 1989 Giulio
Romano exhibition. It was built from architectural plans now in Düsseldorf and carried out in 1567 by the imperial antiquarian, Mantuan Iacopo Strada. The plates are by architect Giovanni Battista
Bertani, aided by painter Ippolito Andreasi in his perfect drawings
of all the decorative work. Bertani is not likely to have taken his mea-

surements from life, but would have reworked the Giulio Romano plans, as the marginal but significant variations in construction show. The Düsseldorf plates are nonetheless valuable because they offer the visitor a view of the villa as it was prior to the eighteenth century work carried out on it. Some of the major details include: the exterior and interior attic, which add majesty to the elevations and hide the view of the roof; a belvedere built facing the city above the loggia of the Muses; an arcade on the upper floor on the east façade; the absence in the centre of this façade of the pediment built in 1790 to suit neoclassical taste.

Chamber of the Victories

This is the last of the decorated rooms in the itinerary around the square court, although it was one of the first to be decorated. The work was already ahead in February 1528, when Nicolò da Milano was paid for four of the eight "heads". These can be identified as the busts that are grouped in pairs in the frieze, in the centre of four panels of plant shoots in relief, shaped into a cross. The same artist is also paid for two Victories. For obvious stylistic reasons he is also attributed with the four remaining heads and the other two female figures at the corners, which are not, like the Victories, holding a palm and laurel wreath, but a trumpet in each hand, the symbols of Fame. Agostino da Mozzanica takes part (1528) in the painted decoration, which imitates a sophisticated work of semi-precious stones, as the document states: "for having painted a frieze in the said chamber made like grotesques in stone".

The wooden ceiling is painted and decorated with figures. In the centre is the Gonzaga shield pre-1530, in confirmation of the dating of the work carried out in the room. In the octagonal corner coffers, four foreshortened brackets meet in the centre to support

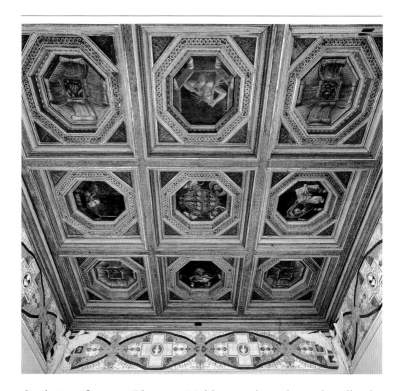

the device of mount Olympus. Unlike anywhere else in the villa, the other four coffers contain scenes of everyday life, seemingly unconnected to any particular meaning, certainly not celebratory: an old lady removing fleas from a child, a woman hanging out a shirt to dry, a young girl combing her hair and another approaching a vase of carnations on the balcony. The invention has a famous precedent in the Bridal Chamber in palazzo Ducale in its daring foreshortening and vase on the parapet of the balcony.

The Permanent Collection
in the West Wing Loft

After passing through a bare room we reach the corridor that leads, to the right, to the courtyard of Honour if we continue our visit to the apartment of the Secret Garden, or to the left to go to the upper floor. The first floor rooms, originally used for storage and the servants' quarters now house very different collections, nevertheless related directly or indirectly to Mantua.

In the first three rooms is the *Mondadori Donation*, with 19 paintings by Federico Zandomeneghi and 13 by Armando Spadini. These fine works were collected by Arnoldo Mondadori and were bequeathed to the museum by his heirs in tribute to the publisher's Mantuan origins. It is the largest collection of works by both artists and as such it represents a particularly important reference point for scholars and enthusiasts. Venetian by birth, Federico Zandomeneghi studied in Florence where he moved from his experience as a Macchiaioli to a style of painting imbued with realist and social content. In 1874, now living in Paris, he joined the Impressionists and was particularly close to the art of Degas, a personal friend. Among the works present, especially worthy of note are *At the Café*, *The Bunch of Flowers*, oil on canvas, and the first-rate pastels *The Lesson* and *The Awakening*. The artistic and personal life of Armando Spadini (1883–1925) was very different. A Florentine initially influenced by the painting of the Macchiaioli, he then moved through a period of Symbolism to reach at the end of his brief life, a personal interpretation of Impressionism aimed at studying the various aspects of everyday domestic life. He worked in Rome and the settings of his paintings are the home, while family members and animals provide the subjects, as can be seen in most of the luminous and affectionate examples present.

Federico
Zandomeneghi,
The Awakening,
detail

Federico
Zandomeneghi,
The Awakening

Armando Spadini,
*Children in the
Open Air*

Armando Spadini,
The Morning

The room in the south-west corner hosts the *"Ugo Sissa" Mesopotamic Collection.* It was loaned to the museum by the heirs of Mantuan Ugo Sissa, a great architect, painter, photographer and essayist who held the prestigious post of Chief Architect in Bagdad between 1953 and 1958. His collection, one of the very few public ones of Mesopotamic art in Italy, comprises some 250 pieces. It is also significant for the broad time span it covers, from the end of the VI millennium BC to the end of the I millennium AD. Some of the most interesting material includes tablets engraved with cuneiform characters, a brick with the seal of king Nebuchadnezzar, amulets and votive statuettes.

Once out of the room we pass into the west wing loft, crossing a bridge that gives us a view of the extrados of Giulio's vaults and an opportunity to study their brickwork, reinforced by iron chains. Either end of the bridge and on both sides are showcases with the *Sezione Gonzaghesca.* The collection contains important examples of

Bushel, 1416

Measure unit
for bricks

cultural history mostly linked to the city of the Gonzaga. It begins with the *Weights and Measures Collection*, with sample units of weights and measures (length and capacity) used by the Mantuan state. The oldest piece, a bushel dated 1416 with Gothic ornamentation, and the 22 examples dated 1554 are all finely cast in bronze and beautifully decorated. It is interesting to note how the government authorities established precise units of measurement for a very wide range of goods, from oil for burning to wine, flour, bricks and roof tiles. Half way along the bridge starts the Coin Section with its almost six hundred coins, which wonderfully documents the output of the Mantuan mint from the thirteenth to the eighteenth century. Mantuan coinage is renowned for its variety and beauty, as well as for the quality of the minting. The right-hand side showcases house a selection of minting dies used to strike Mantua's coins and medals both at the time of the Gonzaga and for the later Austrian government. The vertical cases contain the most valuable coins and medals in the collection.

We now move on the first room in the north wing, which houses the *"Giuseppe Acerbi" Egyptian Collection*. Giuseppe Acerbi, a distinguished Mantuan (from Castel Goffredo), was Austrian consul in Egypt. In 1829 he took part in several stages of the famous archaeological expedition led by Jean François Champollion, the man who deciphered hieroglyphics. Between the end of the 1820s and the early thirties he put together an important collection of archaeological material which in 1840 he bequeathed to the city of Mantua. Before entering the collection, entirely on view, there is a small explanatory room. In the first room, of particular interest are the *sculptures*, some of which bear hieroglyphics with royal scrolls;

the large bronze head of queen *Arsinoe*, bride of Ptolemy III; amulets
with frequent depictions of sacred animals and deities; *shuebte*, statuettes used as substitutes for the deceased so that they could per-
form their tasks in the kingdom of the dead; Canopic alabaster vas-
es; a *bronze cat*, one of the largest and best proportioned known.

From the Fisheries to the Secret Garden

The fish ponds and east façade

If we descend the stairs near the Egyptian collection and cross the courtyard, we return to the loggia of David by way of the bridge over the fisheries. These are made up of two communicating ponds separated by the bridge. During the summer season the fish could "withdraw into the shade" of the niches open on all sides, as Iacopo Strada demonstrates to us. The fisheries separate the palazzo from the garden, and the water that laps the rusticated podium gives the building an emphasis and appeal that only a direct relationship with water can provide, as in the aristocratic houses of Venice. The façade has very visible and deliberate asymmetries: an uneven succession of pillars and columns supporting the four Serlian motifs on either side; but the mirror effect of the composition and the reflecting of the whole in the ponds turns any dissonance to harmony. The balconies in front of each french window allow the view between interior and exterior to continue, and throw light evocatively on the frescoes and stucco work. The continuous upper balcony was originally a loggia, removed during the late-eighteenth century restoration work when the pediment, still visible, was added to the central body. The bridge over the fish ponds has twelve marble pillars that once belonged to a fountain of which there are no records: the flared upper part meets up with masks whose open mouths spurted jets of water.

The garden and other buildings

This was the villa's largest and most important garden, surrounded in turn by other enclosed gardens. There are not enough surviving pictures or descriptions to reconstruct it, though. Looking

northwards towards the present day exit, we see the part of the building at the end of the fish pond that nowadays is the bookshop and café. Embellished with fountains, few traces of which remain, there was once a chapel here and the hydraulic machinery that worked the fountains and water displays. Farther to the right, at the end of the boundary wall, is the apartment of the Secret Garden, mentioned further on; this is echoed on the east side by a symmetrical building that once served as the gardener's lodgings. The two buildings are connected by a stage-like exedra, probably added in 1651 by the duke's architect Nicolò Sebregondi. Contemporary to the exedra is the long building that encloses the garden to the south. Now used to host large exhibitions, in the past the more delicate ornamental plants and citruses were sheltered here in the winter: its name *Fruttiere* indicates its original use. Farther to the right is a building running beside the fish ponds and standing symmetrically to where the chapel and waterworks once were. It is thought to have been built in the seventeenth century as a stables. Nowadays a conference hall, still visible under the stairs is the old cobblestone floor with its central lane and the stumps of the marble columns that separated the horses' stalls.

Apartment of the Secret Garden

Although the villa itself was a refuge for the prince to cultivate his "honest leisure" in his free time, as the dedication in the chamber of Psyche reads, Federico felt the need for an even more intimate secret garden. He undoubtedly wished to emulate the delightful secret garden of his mother Isabella d'Este in Palazzo Ducale, a place for learned conversation, contemplation and rest. The Large chamber no longer has its original vault, once frescoed by Giulio's assistants, and it is not part of the visit. We enter an elongated octagonal Vestibule, with a pavilion vault decorated with fine grotesques probably by Luca di Faenza. In the ribbing is a comprehensive repertory of real and imaginary animals typical of grotesques; the mount Olympus device appears twice. In the central octagon under a pergola of grapes, among dignitaries and a range of animals, the harvesting putti seem to recall the ancient theme of the cult of Bacchus. The floor is a mosaic decorated with variously coloured river pebbles. The door opposite the entrance leads into the spacious chamber of Attilius Regulus, with late eighteenth century floor, fireplace and geometric wall decorations. The vault is instead decorated with the original frescoes and stucco work with the main theme, on a moral tone, expressed in the central octagon where an *Allegory of the Prince's Virtues Appears*. The debate over the exact interpretation of the figures is still open; however the general meaning would appear to be: at the top, a *Victory* (with palms) and a *Victorious War* (cuirass and palm) flying towards three female figures, perhaps alluding to the *Arts*. The latter are about to be crowned by another figure holding a book, perhaps *History*, and *Mercury*, god of commerce and prosperity seems to be inviting everyone to follow him. On the left, a young girl with a setsquare can be identified as the *Perfect Work*. She is holding Olympus in one hand, to imply that Federico's reign is virtuous and prosperous. The rest of the vault is subdivided into four pentagonal segments separated by as many vertical strips. The iconography in the pentagons, starting from the pendentive diametrically opposite the entrance and moving leftwards, reads: *The torture of Attilius Regulus*. The Roman general was taken prisoner by the Carthaginians and was sent to Rome to try to gain peace. Once in Rome, though, he asked for the war to continue; he then returned to Carthage, as he had promised, well knowing that death awaited him. He was tortured in a barrel filled with nails. *The Judgement of Zaleuch.* Legislator of Locride in ancient Greece, Zaleuch issued a law that condemned adulterers to be blinded. His son was discovered committing adultery and to reconcile his fatherly love with his respect for the law the legislator-judge ordered only one of his son's eyes to be removed and he offered his own eye in compensation. *The mercy of Alexander.* After a terrible storm that hit the army in the Samarcanda hills, a confused soldier numb from the cold sat on the throne of Alexander the Great to warm himself by the fire. Although his act was a treasonable offence, the king kept the soldier on the throne and offered him his cloak. *Horace Coclitis.* The brave soldier saved Rome by single-handedly defending the Sublicius bridge against Etruscan attackers while his companions demolished it behind him. Despite his wounds he managed to jump to safety in the Tiber. The vertical rectangles contain the virtues that seem to refer to the scenes illustrated. Zaleuch is preceded by *Justice*, Alexander by *Charity*, Horace Coclitis by *Fortitude*. Attilius Regulus is accompanied by a female figure shrouded in a veil which makes her intangible; she stands like a demure Venus, with a dragon at her side. Since the dragon essentially signifies guardianship (if one thinks of the dragons guarding the source of the river Styx in the chamber of Amor and Psyche), it may be a virtue relating to the concept of keeping one's given word. In the centre of the walls, between two brackets, stucco low-relief works also illustrate the three virtues accompanied by two putti with their relative attributes. In the panel on the side opposite the entrance there is a female figure with

the Olympus device, a putto with a dog and one with an A: three of Federico's devices. Proceeding to the right, we find: *Charity, Fortitude* and *Prudence*. The subject matter in this room, together with that in the other rooms causes one to reflect on the over-hasty definitions of palazzo Te as a place dedicated entirely to pleasure. In actual fact both the moulded and painted decorations range from cultural topics to erotic and political ones, in keeping with the complex and totalising view of Renaissance man in constant dialogue with the classical tradition and symbology dear to the Christian west. There are no records about this decoration, although the work on the apartment can be dated to the 1520s (Oberhuber). Some authors see the hand of Primaticcio in the Zaleuch fresco, partly because drawings of this scene were certainly taken to France by the artist. However, attribution cannot be confirmed due to the scarcity of references to contemporary autograph painting by Primaticcio. The stuccoes can be likened to the work of Giovan Battista Mantovano.

Loggia

After returning to the vestibule and turning left we reach the Loggia, which overlooks the Secret Garden that lends its name to the apartment. The three apertures are supported by two half-columns at ei-

Loggia of the Secret Garden. South wall

Loggia of the Secret Garden. The vault, *Apotheosis of the Soul*

ther end, and by two central columns of lumachella marble, damaged by the weather. The tripartite decoration occupies the vault and walls. On the barrel vault and in the lunettes are scenes from a story that can be generally understood but has not yet been convincingly linked to any written source. The first episode is in the lower right-hand panel next to the corner opposite the entrance; here we see the *Birth* of a child aided by Diana Ephesia, goddess of births, while a spirit is lighting a torch as a symbol of life beginning. To the right, *The suckling*, as the family eats its meals, then *Work* in the fields and, in the lunette, *Rest* from hard labour in the countryside. Continuing in the outer band: *Falling in love*, with merrymaking and dances among the young; *War*, *Infirmity*, represented by a sick man on whom blood-letting is being practiced with glass cups, while others are preparing for examination and cure. In the next lunette is a *Sacrifice to Jupiter*, perhaps linked to the man's infirmity, or to be seen generally as an expression of religiousness. The nearby panel in the central row shows the *Death* of the elderly man, with the extinguished torch abandoned on the ground. At the other end, *Fame*, at the top, and *Notoriety* compete for the memory of the deceased, whose soul, as the central panel shows, is already shining in a celestial *Apotheosis*. All the scenes are surrounded by frames

89

painted with floral motifs containing panels, roundels and lozenges with small stucco decoration. The wall in front of the entrance has a walled-up door flanked by panels with imaginative grotesques surrounding a medallion; the motif is repeated with delightful variations in the small figures that populate the plant shoots in the grotesques on the other walls. The subject matter in the medallions, painted on a dark red background, starting from the wall in front, is: *Pruning*, the goddess *Earth, Silenus drinking from a goatskin, Silenus sleeping, Satyr milking a goat, Satyr and nymph.* The long wall is tripartite, like the loggia; in the centre of the sides is a painted scene framed in stucco: to the left *Silenus on the chariot*, inspired by a classical marble housed in palazzo Ducale; to the right *Bacchus and Ariadne*. The centre band is dominated by a long, poorly conserved painting of a procession of sea gods celebrating the marriage of Peleus and Thetis. The top band is enlivened by simulated recesses and projections, with grotesques and small figures on differently coloured backgrounds; in the centre is a roundel with the Olympus device. The decorative pattern is repeated in the lower band and the device in the centre is the small wood (boschetto). In this case too, no records remain of the accounts, which makes it hard to provide certain dating and attribution. Oberhuber suggests 1528–1529 for the vault, possibly a little early. Agreement with the scholar about the prevailing presence of Anselmo Guazzi in the painting of the figures can be confirmed, while the grotesques can be likened to those in the chamber of the Grotesques documented as   The Secret Garden

being by Luca da Faenza. The loggia has a cobble floor similar to the one in the vestibule. It is divided into compartments decorated with Gongaza emblems; among these the device of the oak with the motto *robore sistit,* belonging to duke Vincenzo Gonzaga (1587–1612), moves the dating forward.

Garden

The right-hand side wall of the loggia and the one opposite were once painted with simulated perspectives, of which vague traces remain. The surviving decoration concerns the frieze on the three highest walls, interrupted by alternating herms and alcoves. These, eighteen in all, were alternately frescoed or stuccoed with subjects taken from Aesop's fables and the monument dedicated to one of Federico's little dogs. Most of the frescoes have disappeared or a great deal is missing, while the stuccoes are better conserved. The niches are framed with moulded friezes and in the two lower corners a device is repeated. The fables with their respective devices start from the outer wall of the loggia, proceeding from left to right on the other walls as well. 1- *The donkey and the dog*, sun; 2- (fable faded), crucible; 3- *Monument to Federico Gonzaga's dog*, Olympus; 4- (fable faded), salamander; 5- *The lion and the mouse* (?), turale dove; 6- (fable faded), glove; 7- *The fox and the crow*, dog; 8- (fable faded), young deer; 9- *The fox and the stork*, hands praying; 10- (fable faded), policies of good luck; 11- *The horse and the lion*, letter A with small flames; 12- (fable faded), belt; 13- *The fly and the bald man*, stirrups; 14- *The dog with a piece of meat*, wheel; 15- *The wolf and the sculpted head*, muzzle; 16- (fable faded), palm branches; 17- *The lion and the shepherd*, winged thunderbolt; 18- *The shepherd and the wolf*, tower. The moulded stucco plant shoot frames are very similar to those in the Large chamber (not on the tour), where work was taking place in 1531: the date can therefore be taken as a reference for the work in the garden. The stuccoes, well executed with solid and broad plasticity are treated with humour, at times slightly coarsely, in a way we saw to be characteristic of Giovan Battista Mantovano.

Grotto

In the façade opposite the loggia an entrance made of natural rocks leads into the Grotto, added by Vincenzo Gonzaga after 1595 and completed during the sovereignty of his son, duke Ferdinando (1612–1626). It is both a homage to the fashion of the time, especially in the milieu of the Medici, and a revisiting of the classical nymphaeum, a source of water dedicated to the nymphs at the end of a garden. The grotto is made up of two connecting rooms ending with an apse containing the remains of a large fountain. It had a great many water displays, as the still existing holes and stretches of piping show, and the niches would have contained sculptures. The decoration is extremely varied in materials and motifs. The walls are lined with coloured rustic stone mosaics or shells, but there are also frames encrusted with mother of pearl, glass surfaces and stuccoes made from coloured mortar. The prevailing elements are the rocky concretions that make it seems like an underground room, and that make way at the top for simulated openings on to a sky dotted with birds and insects. Vasari gives a detailed description of this type of construction, in which "the water trickles through these encrustations of tartar and, dripping, it makes a sweet sound to hear and a delight to see". He also explains how the impression of naturalism can be increased by carefully adding plants to the composition: "grasses are made to grow above this which with an order that seems like disorder and wildness makes them much more natural

The Grotto

The Grotto. Detail
of the vault

The Grotto.
Octagons with the
Story of Alcina

and realistic". In the first room, traces of devices can be seen in the niches; from the one to the left of the door: a phoenix, two Cs linked together, a crucible, a crescent moon with the motto SIC. In the second room, on the vault are three scenes from the story of Alcina, taken from the 5th book of *Orlando Furioso* by Ludovico Ariosto. From the bottom left we see: 1- the sorceress capturing fish "with simple words and pure magic"; Astolfo sees Alcina and falls in love with her; 3- Alcina persuades Astolfo to climb on to a small island which is really a whale. The two depart and Rinaldo vainly dives into the sea to try and stop them. The niches below contain symbols linked to the four basic elements of the universe. Like the scenes from Ariosto, they refer to the transformation of matter, either by magic or a knowledge of alchemy. The flowering plant signifies the earth, a burning crater, fire, a bird, air, and a dolphin, water.